DIVING
CAYMAN ISLANDS

DIVING CAYMAN ISLANDS

BY JESSE CANCELMO

AQUA QUEST PUBLICATIONS, INC. ■ NEW YORK

PUBLISHER'S NOTE

The Aqua Quest *Diving* series offers extensive information on dive sites as well as topside activities.

At the time of publication, the information contained in this book was determined to be as accurate and up-to-date as possible. The reader should bear in mind, however, that dive site terrain and landmarks change due to weather or construction. In addition, new dive shops, restaurants, hotels and stores can open and existing ones close. Telephone numbers are subject to change as are government regulations.

The publisher welcomes the reader's comments and assistance to help ensure the accuracy of future editions of this book.

Good diving and enjoy your stay!

Library of Congress Cataloging-in-Publication Data

Cancelmo, Jesse.
    Diving Cayman Islands / by Jesse Cancelmo.
    p.   cm.   — (Aqua Quest diving series)
    Includes index.
    ISBN 1-881652-10-6 : $18.95
    1. Scuba diving—Cayman Islands—Guidebooks. 2.
Cayman Islands—Guidebooks. I. Title. II. Series
GV838.673.C37C36 1997
797.2'3—dc21
                                       97-8606
                                         CIP

Cover: Divers from around the globe visit the Cayman Islands to experience the shear, breathtaking wall dives such as Bloody Bay's Lea Lea's Lookout site on Little Cayman.

Title page: Schools of silvery horse-eye jacks swirl through Little Cayman's Jackson's Reef feeding on small fish.

Printed in Hong Kong
10 9 8 7 6 5 4 3 2 1

Design by Richard Liu.

ACKNOWLEDGEMENTS

I wish to thank Susan Young for her invaluable help with the Grand Cayman material and for her special contribution to the dining section; Danny Jetmore and Ed Beaty for their discerning review of the Cayman Brac chapter; Laurie Gotterup for her enthusiastic support and insights with the Little Cayman material; special thanks also to Jill Rabjohn and Anthony Carnaxide.

DEDICATION

To Sarah and Jess Cancelmo,
my future scuba buddies.

Contents

FOREWORD

Grand Cayman is perhaps the single most popular island for scuba diving in the entire Western Hemisphere. The visitors, many of whom return year after year, come for the exciting marine life and incredible variety of dive sites. There are more than a hundred dive sites surrounding Grand Cayman alone and new ones are added every year. Dramatic wall dives can be experienced nearly anywhere off the island's perimeter; inshore shallow reef dives for "second dives" feature friendly fishes and fascinating critters; and numerous shore dives are easily accessible. Cayman reefs abound in Caribbean sea life. Divers who live for marine life interaction can experience rays, turtles, moray eels and large friendly groupers at various Cayman sites.

Grand Cayman is by far the most visited, yet it is only one facet of the Cayman trio. The much smaller Cayman Brac offers a relaxed, friendly, more traditional island atmosphere with many of the resort amenities found on the big island. There's miles of pristine reefs and dramatic drop-offs that few divers have ever seen.

Little Cayman, once the "outpost" of the Caymans, is still off the traveler's mainstream. It's secluded but comfortable. Bloody Bay Wall maintains its reputation as the most sensational wall dive in the Caribbean. The profusion and variety of life there and on other Little Cayman reefs are simply awesome.

Each of the three Caymans has their distinct flavor and to fully appreciate the Cayman Island experience, you should visit all of them.

In addition to covering more than 87 dive sites, *Diving Cayman Islands* provides essential information on touring, accommodations, shopping, dining and night life.

Jesse Cancelmo
Houston, Texas
November 1997

CHAPTER I THE CAYMANS

Turtling to Tourism

THE PAST

The Cayman Islands were first sighted by Christopher Columbus during his final voyage to the New World. He was so impressed by the abundance of sea turtles that he named the islands Las Tortugas (The Turtles). Columbus was far off his course from Hispaniola to Panama when he passed by the two smaller Caymans in 1503. Decades later the Cayman Islands were given their present name after the crocodiles also found there (Cayman means crocodile in Carib).

Cayman's turtles had few predators before the arrival of European sailors. Although young hatchlings have a low survival rate, only sharks were a threat once they have matured. While there was little on these low coral islands to attract settlers, for seafarers the fresh green turtle meat was in high demand for the long return voyage to Europe. Soon the Caymans became a popular stopping point for the trade routes of the Spanish Main. Live turtles, turtle eggs and fresh water were taken on board. Live turtles were turned on their backs for storage and safekeeping. A 600-pound (272 kg) turtle could survive for nearly a year without food or water. Turtle meat provided a safe and abundant source of protein. As turtles were exported to Europe, turtle soup became a culinary delicacy. Tortoise shell combs and other items made from turtle shells became fashionable, increasing further the demand for turtles.

Turtling continued as an important enterprise in the Cayman Islands. But as the turtle population dwindled, the Cayman captains were forced to head farther and farther away— first toward Cuba, then south to the turtle nesting grounds near the cays of Nicaragua.

The Cayman Islands were eventually claimed by the British and settled by soldiers from Jamaica in the mid-1600s. The inhabitants survived on turtling, fishing, farming and wrecking. Wreckers made a living off the spoils of ships that had the misfortune of hitting the shallow reefs near shore. Some of the wrecks occurred by accident; others were reportedly encouraged by lights placed on shore by wreckers.

In the late 17th and early 18th centuries, pirates, buccaneers and freebooters found food, water and refuge in the Caymans. The notorious Sir Henry Morgan, Edward Teach who was more popularly known as Blackbeard, and other infamous yet colorful characters made these island their home. To this day, tales are told of hidden treasure and unclaimed caches and booty. Legend also has it that direct descendants of Blackbeard and his many wives still live on the islands.

Later in the 18th century, Caymanians exported mahogany, and traded coffee, corn, sugarcane, plantains and coconuts. The local mahogany trees enabled a small yet prosperous shipbuilding industry. The famous "Cayman schooners" were hand-fashioned from this strong hardwood.

New churches and schools were built in the 19th century and although still technically part of Jamaica, the Caymanians were left pretty much alone to fend for themselves and handle their own government issues. As the population grew, more and more Caymanians went to sea to make their living as merchant mariners.

The year 1957 marked a milestone for Grand Cayman when the Cuban-born, ex-merchant marine Bob Soto returned to Grand Cayman to start the island's first scuba diving operation. At

Sponges like this iridescent tube sponge are good places to find critters such as brittle stars, gobies and blennies that often take refuge in their cavities.

that time tourism was in its infancy and the Bay View and Pageant Beach Yacht Club were the only two hotels on the entire island. Bob secured a concession at the Pageant Beach and with a new hand-built boat, a military surplus air compressor, and some converted fire extinguishers with homemade backpacks, he was ready for his first customers.

In the mid-1960s, Cayman emerged as a major Caribbean dive destination. By the 70s, the influx of divers was spiraling to unforeseen numbers. The year-round warm, crystal clear, fish-filled waters became an international diving discovery.

The hordes of sea turtles that once filled the Cayman waters were sorely diminished by the middle of the twentieth century. But the Caymanians didn't forget them. In 1958 this symbol of Cayman history was included on the islands' Coat of Arms above the inscription, "He Hath Founded It Upon The Seas". Government conservation measures were taken and in 1968 the Cayman Turtle Farm was established. This private endeavor resulted from a marine biologist who saw the potential for financing research by marketing turtle products. When the United States banned the importation of turtle goods in 1978, the emphasis changed from turtle products to breeding and research. Within 10 years, young turtles from the farm were being released into Cayman waters. The Cayman Turtle Farm currently replenishes the Cayman Islands with more than 4,000 hatchlings and yearlings each year.

THE PRESENT

The Cayman Islands, comprised of Grand Cayman, Cayman Brac and Little Cayman, are a British Crown Colony located in the northwestern Caribbean Sea. The main island lies 500 miles (807 km) south of Miami and 200 miles (323 km) west of Jamaica. The smaller sister islands, Cayman Brac and Little Cayman, lie 80 miles (129 km) east of Grand Cayman and are separated by a channel seven miles (11 km) wide.

Approximately 28,000 full time residents live on Grand Cayman which is 22 miles (36 km) long and 8 miles (13 km) across. More than 90 percent of the tourists visit Grand Cayman's Seven Mile Beach where modern high rise hotels and condominiums line the island's main attraction. West Bay, a small town and residential district north of Seven Mile Beach, is noted for picturesque churches, shops and bungalow homes. The south coastline between Savannah and Bodden Town retains the old island character and history. The Midland and Eastern Districts are the least populated areas on the island.

Today there are more than 40 scuba operators on Grand Cayman alone and the tens of thousands of scuba divers who visit are a major contribution to the island's economy. Along with offshore banking and finance, tourism has enabled Cayman to rapidly develop as one of the richest islands in the Caribbean.

George Town, the islands' capital, is now a major offshore finance center and has more than 500 banks and 300 insurance companies.

Cayman Brac, shaped like a pea pod, is 12 miles (19 km) long and a mile (1.6 km) wide. The west end is flat and near sea level, but the elevation steadily increases going eastward to a maximum height of 140 feet (42 m) at the eastern tip where the limestone bluff drops in a sheer cliff to meet the ocean. About 14,500 full time residents known as "Brackers" live on the island; most occupy the north side. Cayman Brac has an attractive combination of tranquility, charm and creature comforts. It's not as far off the beaten path as Little Cayman, yet it's a time-warp away from the bustle of Grand Cayman's Seven Mile Beach. Cayman Brac has two modern resorts, a jet airport, car rentals and a few local restaurants. The Brac's topside diversions include two small villages, a museum and several interesting caves.

Little Cayman, located seven miles (11 km) west of Cayman Brac, is only a tad bit smaller than the sister island. The "hideaway island" of the threesome has approximately 100 full time residents on its 10 square miles (26 sq km). Except for a small bluff near the east end, Little Cayman is basically flat with dense mangrove forests. A reef-fringed lagoon allows protection for boats on the south shore. There are also several brackish ponds on the island the largest of which, just east of the airstrip, hosts a variety of birds and wildlife.

Little Cayman is a haven for divers and salt water fishermen alike. Besides the world class diving, there's sensational fishing in the flats for tarpon, permit and bone. The simplicity and quiet of Little Cayman draw naturalists

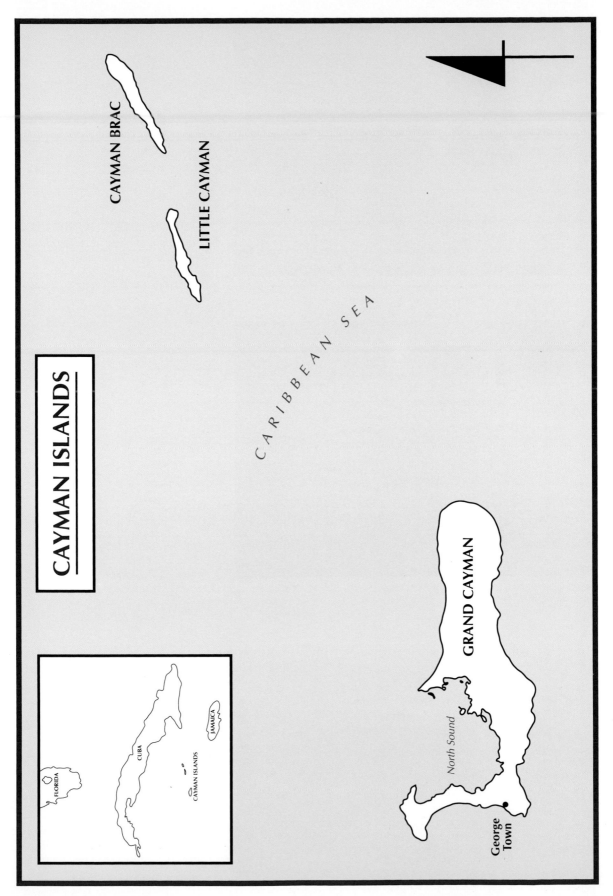

CAYMAN ISLANDS

CAYMAN BRAC

LITTLE CAYMAN

CARIBBEAN SEA

GRAND CAYMAN

North Sound

George Town

FLORIDA

CUBA

JAMAICA

CAYMAN ISLANDS

The genuine warmth and friendliness of Caymanians is reflected in the smiling faces of these East End children.

Vines of colorful bougainvillea grow wild on fences and along many roadsides in Grand Cayman.

The Pink House is a traditional Caymanian home featuring pastel colors, a metal roof, gingerbread trim and a sandy yard with tropical shrubs.

FESTIVALS AND CELEBRATIONS

Batabano, a colorful and exhilarating musical festival with an Eastern Caribbean flavor, is an annual celebration that takes place on Grand Cayman a week before Easter. Activities include parades with fancy floats, steel bands and dancers in exotic costumes. There's local foods and street dancing all weekend long. **Bracchanal** is a similar celebration held each May in Cayman Brac.

Pirate's Week National Festival, Cayman's largest and most popular island celebration, occurs in late October. This week-long festival commemorates Cayman's legendary scoundrels and visitors come from afar to party. Firework displays and costume parades are part of the festivities .

Taste of Cayman is a culinary event that takes place in July. The Cayman Island Restaurant Association organizes a chili cook-off, fair and fireworks. This is one weekend that Cayman chefs get to really show their stuff!

Every June, the **Queen's Birthday** is duly celebrated in a colonial atmosphere of pomp and British flavor. Featured are a parade, marching bands and gun salutes.

---

from around the world.

Recent modernizations on Little Cayman include telephones, central power, air conditioning, rental jeeps, a new restaurant and a tiny shopping center with a Cayman Bank branch.

The Cayman Islands are a story of success for the people and the environment. A role model for other developing islands around the world, Grand Cayman expanded its infrastructure, developed tourism and business while caring for its natural resources. Caymanians now enjoy the highest standard of living in the Caribbean.

The Cayman turtle is more than a symbol of its heritage. It also represents a "can do" attitude for Cayman conservation and marine management efforts.

USEFUL INFORMATION

Climate. The Caymans are a year-round destination and the weather is exceptionally stable from May through December. Winter air temperatures in the Caymans range from 70 to 80°F (21-27°C). In the summer the temperature varies between 80 and 90°F (27-32°C) during the day. The summer water temperature usually stays steady at 85°F (29°C) and only drops to about 77 to 80°F (25-27°C) during the winter months.

Currency. The official currency is the Cayman Dollar (CI$) which is equal to US$1.25 (or US$1.00 equals CI$0.80). United States dollars are accepted throughout the Cayman Islands. Goods and services are usually priced in Cayman dollars. All of the major hotels and most restaurants and stores accept major credit cards.

Dress Suggestions. Casual, comfortable attire is the norm in the Caymans, even at the most elegant eateries in Grand Cayman. Bring clothing that is light and loose fitting. Swimsuits are fine on the beach, aboard boats and around the hotels, but most shops and restaurants expect shoes and a shirt. A lightweight rain poncho can be handy for the brief tropical showers that are common throughout the Caribbean.

Duty and Restrictions. The duty-free limit for

Cruise ship passengers disembark to shop in George Town, visit Grand Cayman's beaches, and snorkel or dive in its crystal-clear waters.

United States citizens is $400. Anything over $400 is subject to a 10 percent duty. The United States bans the import of Cayman parrots and turtle products, even those from the Turtle Farm. Enforcement is strict.

Electricity. Electricity on the islands is 110 volts 60 cycles, the same as in the United States.

Entry and Exit Requirements. Americans and Canadians visiting the Cayman Islands will need proof of citizenship (birth certificate, voter's registration or passport), a photo ID, a return ticket and a completed immigration form. A tax of US$10 (CI$8) is collected on departure from all visitors 12 years and older. It is advisable to reconfirm all return reservations at least 48 hours prior to departure.

Getting There. Grand Cayman is only one and a quarter hours by air from Miami and about two and a half hours from Houston. Cayman Airways has several daily flights to

Grand Cayman from Miami and nonstop jet service from Atlanta, Houston, Orlando and Tampa. Northwest Airlines, United, USAir, American Airlines and American Trans Air service Grand Cayman from various United States gateways. Cayman Air offers daily jet service between Grand Cayman and Cayman Brac; Island Air has small propeller plane service between all three islands. Flight schedules are subject to frequent change. Also note that Island Air has a baggage weight limit (45 pounds/person). The charge for overweight luggage is 50 cents per pound.

Cayman Brac has a jet runway and a modern air terminal. Little Cayman has a 3,300-foot-long grass landing strip (no tower or lights) that can handle most small prop planes.

Island Transportation. Taxi service on Grand Cayman is excellent. As an alternative, cars, jeeps, vans, motorbikes or bicycles can be rented. A valid driver's license and a Cayman Island visitor's driving permit are needed to drive on the islands. Permits can be obtained at the rental agency for a nominal fee of around CI$4. Remember to drive on the left side of the road.

There are a few taxis for hire on Cayman Brac. Cars, scooters and bicycles can be rented there also. Little Cayman now has a jeep rental agency. All the resorts there provide bicycles for their guests.

Language. English is the spoken language throughout this British Crown Colony. The distinctive Caymanian accent is a pleasant mix of Caribbean British, lilted Welsh with a slight influence from the southern United States.

Medical. There's a hospital in George Town, Grand Cayman and the small Faith Hospital in Cayman Brac. For emergencies, call 555 or 911. The nearest hyperbaric chamber, a two-patient double lock, is at the Grand Cayman hospital (call 555).

Postage Rates. It costs 15 cents (CI) to send a postcard to the United States or Canada. Post offices are located in George Town and in the West Shore Center, West Bay Road.

Telephone. Cayman has direct dialing service to the United States, the United Kingdom and Europe. AT&T and MCI calling cards can be used for overseas calls. Local calls are on a seven-digit system. When dialing direct from the United States, use area code 345.

Time. The Cayman Islands are on Eastern Standard Time but do not observe Daylight Savings. In the summer, Cayman time is the same as Houston and Chicago (Central Daylight Savings).

Water. Drinking water quality is excellent throughout the Caymans.

The Cayman Islands has developed into one of the world's largest international banking and finance centers.

CHAPTER II ACCOMMODATIONS

GRAND CAYMAN

Grand Cayman offers a wide range of accommodations from simple guest houses to deluxe 200-room high-rise hotels. The largest concentration of hotels and condos are along the famous stretch of Seven Mile Beach, north of George Town. Hyatt, Radisson, Westin, Ramada and Holiday Inn are some of the familiar names seen there. There are also smaller, more intimate hotels, guest houses, condos and beachside villas south of George Town, on the north shore and on the far East End. Many prefer the dedicated dive resorts while others opt for the flexibility of staying in one of Grand Cayman's modern beachside condominiums.

CAYMAN BRAC

Cayman Brac has two dedicated dive resorts, the Divi Tiara Beach Resort and the Brac Reef Beach Resort. Both are situated on prime south shore beach front and are minutes from the airport. Condominium and house rental options are also available in Cayman Brac.

LITTLE CAYMAN

Little Cayman has three cozy little dive resorts—Pirate's Point, Sam McCoy's and Southern Cross—as well as the recently constructed Little Cayman Beach Resort. All four resorts are situated on the water near the west end. Other options in Little Cayman include The Village Inn, Paradise Villas, the Seaview Villa, The Conch Club Condos and several house rentals.

LIVEABOARDS

Two liveaboard dive boats operate in the Cayman Islands. The *Cayman Aggressor III* docks in George Town, Grand Cayman and the *Little Cayman Diver II* berths in Cayman Brac.

The *Cayman Aggressor III* is 110 feet (33 m) long and handles a maximum of 18 divers. The boat is well-equipped and has a spacious main deck and sun deck. It also has special shelves for storing cameras and strobes and an on-board E-6 slide processing system. The *Cayman Aggressor III* reaches the remote sites at the north and east ends of Grand Cayman and when weather permits, travels to the legendary sites at Little Cayman. The open ocean crossing takes about six hours.

The *Little Cayman Diver II* visits Little Cayman sites exclusively. This 90-foot-long (27 m) luxury motor yacht has five cabins with private baths and is designed to comfortably accommodate 10 divers. The *Little Cayman Diver II* has a spacious lounge with a 31-inch screen TV and a separate galley and wheelhouse.

Knobby soft corals extend their polyps to feed on drifting plankton in the Caymans' nutrient-rich currents.

	Rooms/Units	Air Conditioning	Tennis	Beach	Pool	Restaurant	Bar	Dive Operation	Gear Storage
GRAND CAYMAN									
7 Mile Beach Hotels									
Beach Club Colony Tel: (345) 949-8100	41	■	■	■	■	■	■	■	
Caribbean Club Tel: (345) 945-4099	18	■		■	■				
Cayman Islander Hotel Tel: (345) 949-0990	64	■			■	■	■	■	■
Clarion Grand Pavillion Tel: (345) 945-5656	93	■	■		■	■	■	■	
Holiday Inn Tel: (345) 945-4444	213	■		■	■	■	■	■	■
Hyatt Regency Tel: (345) 949-1234	236	■	■	■	■	■	■	■	■
Indies Suites Tel: (345) 945-5025	41	■		■	■	■	■	■	■
Radisson Resort Tel: (345) 949-0088	315	■		■	■	■	■	■	
Treasure Island Resort Tel: (345) 949-7777	280	■	■	■	■	■	■	■	
Sleep Inn Hotel Tel: (345) 949-9111	115	■		■	■	■	■	■	■
Westin Casuarina Tel: (345) 945-3800	343	■	■	■	■	■	■	■	■
Windjammer Hotel Tel: (345) 945-4324	12	■				■	■		

	Rooms/Units	Air Conditioning	Tennis	Beach	Pool	Restaurant	Bar	Dive Operation	Gear Storage
7 Mile Beach Condos & Villas									
Anchorage Tel: (345) 945-4088	15	■	■	■	■				
Avalon Tel: (345) 945-4171	27	■	■	■	■				
Beachcomber Tel: (345) 945-4470	24	■		■	■				
Britannia Villas Tel: (345) 949-1234	35	■	■	■	■	■	■	■	
Casa Caribe Tel: (345) 945-4287	24	■	■	■	■				
Cayman Club Tel: (345) 945-5258	24	■	■	■	■				
Cayman Reef Resort Tel: (345) 949-4819	62	■	■	■	■				
Christopher Columbus Tel: (345) 945-4354	30	■	■	■	■				
Colonial Club Tel: (345) 945-4660	24	■	■	■	■				
Coralstone Club Tel: (345) 945-5820	36	■	■	■	■				
Discovery Point Club Tel: (345) 945-4724	45	■	■	■	■				
George Town Villas Tel: (345) 949-5172	54	■	■	■	■				
Grand Bay Club Tel: (345) 945-4728	21	■	■	■	■				

	Rooms/Units	Air Conditioning	Tennis	Beach	Pool	Restaurant	Bar	Dive Operation	Gear Storage
Harbour Heights Tel: (345) 945-4295	46	■	■	■	■				
Heritage Club Tel: (345) 945-4993	18	■	■	■	■				
Island Pine Villas Tel: (345) 949-6586	40	■	■	■	■				
Lacovia Tel: (345) 949-7599	55	■	■	■	■				
London House Tel: (345) 945-4060	21	■	■	■	■				
Palms Condominiums Tel: (345) 945-5291	15	■	■	■	■				
Pan Cayman House Tel: (345) 945-4002	10	■		■					
Plantana Condominiums Tel: (345) 945-4430	49	■		■	■				
Plantation Village Tel: (345) 949-4199	70	■	■	■	■				
Seagull Condominiums Tel: (345) 949-5756	32	■		■					
7 Mile Beach Resort Tel: (345) 949-0332	38	■	■	■	■				
Silver Sands Tel: (345) 949-3343	42	■	■	■	■				
Tamarind Bay Tel: (345) 949-4593	28	■	■	■	■				
Tarquynn Manor Tel: (345) 945-4038	20	■		■	■				

	Rooms/Units	Air Conditioning	Tennis	Beach	Pool	Restaurant	Bar	Dive Operation	Gear Storage
Turtle Beach Villas Tel: (345) 949-6347	23	■		■	■				
Victoria House Tel: (345) 945-4233	26	■	■	■					
Villas of the Galleon Tel: (345) 945-4433	74	■		■					
South Hotels									
Ambassadors Inn Tel: (345) 949-7577	18	■			■	■	■	■	■
Coconut Harbour Tel: (345) 949-7468	35	■			■	■	■	■	■
Pirates Inn Tel: (345) 947-2339	10	■		■				■	■
Sammy's Airport Inn Tel: (345) 945-2100	53	■			■	■	■		
Seaview Hotel Tel: (345) 949-8804	15	■		■	■	■	■	■	■
Sunset House Tel: (345) 949-7111	59	■			■	■	■	■	■
North Hotels									
Cayman Kai Resort Tel: (345) 947-9055	20	■		■	■	■	■	■	■
Magnificent Dive Dump Tel: (345) 949-3787	5	■		■					
Ole Jud's Inn Tel: (345) 947-9333	10	■		■	■	■	■	■	
Retreat at Rum Point Tel: (345) 947-9135	23	■	■	■	■				

	Rooms/Units	Air Conditioning	Tennis	Beach	Pool	Restaurant	Bar	Dive Operation	Gear Storage
Spanish Bay Reef Resort Tel: (345) 949-3765	50	■		■	■	■	■	■	■
East Hotels									
Cayman Diving Lodge Tel: (345) 947-7555	14	■		■		■	■	■	■
Morritt's Tortuga Club Tel: (345) 947-7449	121	■		■	■	■	■	■	
CAYMAN BRAC									
Hotels									
Brac Reef Beach Resort Tel: (345) 948-1323	40	■	■	■	■	■	■	■	■
Divi Tiara Beach Resort Tel: (345) 948-1553	59	■	■	■	■	■	■	■	■
Condos & Villas									
Brac Carib. Reef Village Tel: (345) 948-2265	16	■		■	■	■		■	
Brac Haven Villas Tel: (345) 948-2473	6	■			■				
La Esperanza Tel: (345) 948-0531	5	■				■	■		
LITTLE CAYMAN									
Hotels									
Little Cayman Bch. Resort Tel: (345) 948-1033	32	■	■	■	■	■	■		■
Pirate's Point Resort Tel: (345) 948-1010	10	■		■		■	■	■	■

Condos & Villas	Rooms/Units	Air Conditioning	Tennis	Beach	Pool	Restaurant	Bar	Dive Operation	Gear Storage
Paradise Villas Tel: (345) 948-0001	12	■		■	■	■	■	■	■
Sam McCoy's Fish & Dive Tel: (345) 948-0026	8	■		■	■	■	■	■	■
Southern Cross Club Tel: (345) 948-1099	10	■	■	■	■	■	■	■	■

Many of Grand Cayman's resorts and condos are found along Seven Mile Beach on the west end of the island. This is the Westin Casuarina.

CHAPTER III SHOPPING AND TOURING

GRAND CAYMAN

Grand Cayman's main shopping districts are in George Town and at the plazas along Seven Mile Beach. Both areas are minutes from the airport. Grand Cayman has bargains on Rolex watches, gold coins, jewelry, French perfumes, cosmetics, crystal, china, designer items and other imported finery. The fine jewelry with maritime designs or mounted coins are especially popular. Paintings and sculptures by local artists and duty-free liquor are available.

Grand Cayman has an abundance of above-water natural wonders to photograph and enjoy. A trip to Cayman is not complete without a visit to the **Turtle Farm** in West Bay. This extraordinary farm has dozens of circular pools where thousands of green turtles are bred and raised. Turtles range in size from 6 ounces (.2 kg) to 600 pounds (273 kg). Most are bred for consumption but many are released to replenish the sea. Other attractions at the turtle farm include Cayman iguanas, several colorful parrots and a native flora display.

Another popular west end tourist spot is the small community of **Hell** which was duly named for the horrible-looking field of jagged, blackened limestone rocks. Add some flames and you'd think you were in Hades. There's even a small post office where you can amuse your friends at home with letters postmarked from Hell.

The famous **Pink House** in the West Bay area is another popular photo stop. It is one of several traditional Caymanian homes to see painted with pastel colors, and sporting metal roofs, porches and gingerbread trim. Head east out of George Town for other Grand Cayman sites such as **Pedro's Castle**, built in 1780 and **Bodden Town**, the islands' first capital. An entire day can easily be spent touring the sparsely populated but historic outer districts on Grand Cayman's East End. Discover the undeveloped parts of the main island where there are 17th and 18th century monuments, **bird sanctuaries**, a **bee farm**, **caves**, **ocean blow holes** and miles of **secluded beaches**.

For a Cayman history tour, visit the Cayman Island's **National Museum** that overlooks George Town harbor. Exhibits range from Cayman flora and fauna above and below the water to the semi-precious gemstone, caymanite. Treasure buffs will also enjoy the Cayman Island **Treasure Museum** across from Seven Mile Beach near the Hyatt Hotel.

For a self-guided walking tour of George Town, stop by the tourist information booth for a Cayman map. Take a tour through the past and see monuments, memorials, traditional Caymanian homes and the **Clock Tower** behind town that was built to commemorate King George V.

For a nature walk, visit the 60-acre (24 ha) **Botanical Park** off the east side of Franks Sound Road. It was officially opened by Queen Elizabeth II in February 1994. Indigenous plants, blue iguanas, vitelline warblers, zenaida doves and Cayman parrots can be seen along the mile-long trail.

Cayman submarine excursions include the 46-passenger *Atlantis* sub that makes dives to 100 feet (30 m) on the West Wall south of George Town, and the two Atlantis deep submersibles. Each deep sub handles two passengers and a pilot on an 800-foot (242 m) wall dive.

CAYMAN BRAC

Shopping in Cayman Brac is limited to a few

Basket sponges are common along Cayman walls and reach gigantic proportions.

The Cayman Turtle Farm on Grand Cayman's northwest end uses a system of salt water tanks to raise turtles from small hatchlings to mature adults weighing more than 600 pounds (273 kg). The turtles are mainly grown for consumption, but thousands are released to repopulate Cayman waters. Turtles are presently much more readily seen by divers than a decade ago.

The famous blow holes at the east end of Grand Cayman shoot geysers of seawater skyward as the waves are forced through holes in the ironshore.

Unlike the flat topography of Grand Cayman and Little Cayman, Cayman Brac has a spectacular cacti-rimmed bluff that runs straight down the center of the island.

The bluff at Cayman Brac has several large caves once used as pirate hide-outs, later as hurricane shelters and now serve as tourist attractions.

local craft outlets and hotel gift shops. Shops to visit include Kirk Freeport, Treasure Chest, Carters, NIM (Native Island Made) Things and Ida Lee's Island Jewelry. NIM and Ida Lee's have Caymanite jewelry which is made from hard dolomite, a semi-precious stone found only in the Cayman Islands.

Topside diversions may be few but are definitely unusual. While the other Caymans are basically flat islands, Cayman Brac has a central limestone **bluff** formation rimmed with cacti and palms that rises to a breathtaking sheer cliff line 140 feet (42 m) high above the sea. A small navigational light stands near the cliff's edge on the east end. More than a hundred stalactite-filled caves honeycomb both sides of the bluff (Brac is Gaelic for bluff). Some are accessible at road level; others, like the **Great Cave**, are entered after a challenging climb up the face of the bluff. Legends still abound of unclaimed pirate booty hidden in a cave by the infamous Blackbeard.

Cayman Brac is a rest station for numerous **migratory birds**. Long-tailed tropic birds, peregrine falcons, green parrots and brown boobies are examples of the interesting wildlife found there.

A recently completed mile-long (1.6 km) **nature trail** through a rugged portion of the bluff provides a snapshot of the past. Parrots, iguanas and other Cayman wildlife can be seen or heard.

A visit to the Cayman Brac **Museum** at **Stake Bay**, about midpoint on the north shore, is a must for history buffs. Local tools, antiques and

artifacts are neatly displayed in a quiet, unassuming building (the former government building). The other Brac settlement is **Spot Bay** on the northeast end where most of the "Brackers" reside.

LITTLE CAYMAN

Most who visit Little Cayman do not have shopping at the top of their vacation agenda. It's a kick back and relax, smell the flora type of island. New development in the 90s has produced Little Cayman's first jeep rental agency and a small general store at the Village Square near the airport.

Most of Little Cayman is an unspoiled nature reserve where egrets, herons and other wild birds land where they please, undisturbed. Undisturbed by people, that is. There are, however, regular bird disturbances on the island caused by the "battle of the birds"— frigate versus booby. Instead of hunting for its own food, the overly aggressive frigate bird habitually steals food from the brown boobys. This raucous display of nature attracts birders from around the globe.

An island tour by day and star gazing by night are some of the peaceful pastimes of a Little Cayman visit. Nature hiking, beachcombing, **bonefishing** and **bird watching** are other allures for those who travel there.

When vacationing on the Brac or Little Cayman, consider a day of touring and shopping on Grand Cayman on the tail end of the trip.

CHAPTER IV   DINING AND NIGHT LIFE

GRAND CAYMAN

Dining. Grand Cayman has a wide assortment of restaurants ranging from fine dining to fast food establishments. There are more than 100 eateries in Grand Cayman that feature everything from international and Caribbean delicacies to fast food hamburgers. Restaurant listings can be found in the Cayman Air in-flight magazine as well as in the tourist information pamphlets provided at all hotels and resorts. Reservations are suggested for the more expensive restaurants.

Many of the resorts and hotels have their own restaurants and offer package prices that include meals.

Listed here are some of Grand Cayman's favorite places to dine.

Expensive

Chef Tell's Grand Old House   949-9333

Continental, Caribbean and oriental specialties in an atmosphere of the old South. Elegant dining and sensational desserts that include a tasty Caribbean key lime pie.

Lantana's   945-5595

Wonderful continental food! The executive chef here prepares his menu with a southwestern flair. Caribbean specialties are also served. The cuisine combinations are impressive in taste and presentation. Lantana's desserts are to die for, particularly the apple tart served hot with a caramel sauce and topped with a scoop of Haagen-Daz vanilla ice cream.

Lobster Pot   949-2736

This restaurant is a place to enjoy delightful continental and seafood specialties with a wonderful ocean view.

Ristorante Pappagallo   949-1119

The specialties served here are from northern Italy, but the setting is romantic and tropical in a 14-acre wildlife sanctuary.

The Wharf   949-2231

This top flight restaurant serves continental, seafood and Caribbean dishes at the edge of Seven Mile Beach. You have a choice of dining inside or al fresco in an oceanside setting. The service is excellent.

Moderate

Almond Tree   949-2893

Caribbean seafood specialties are served here in a casual island-style ambiance. A special offered three times a week is an all-you-can-eat Cayman-style fish. The fare is good and the price is great!

Bella Capri   945-4755

If you're not ravishing, you can get excellent traditional Italian cuisine in appetizer portions here. The *gnocchi* is terrific and the *cappuccino* is great.

Early in the morning or late in the day after most of the sun-worshippers have retreated, Seven Mile Beach takes on an especially tranquil, unhurried atmosphere.

Cafe Tortuga Grill & Bar   949-8669

Ribs, chicken, shrimp and pasta delights are served here in a casual, friendly atmosphere.

Captain Morgan's Steak House   949-2333

Captain Morgan's is the only "cook it yourself at the table" restaurant in Cayman. The beef is reputed for being melt-in-your-mouth tender. They also serve chicken and shrimp.

Corita's Copper Kettle   949-2696, 949-7078

Corita's serves excellent traditional Cayman foods such as salt cod and ackee with eggs for breakfast; tasty "fritters" which to Americans look more like a biscuit; Cayman style fish; oxtail and stewed conch. They have two locations.

Crow's Nest   949-9366

Situated on South Sound Road, the Crow's Nest is a charming place to dine. They prepare fresh fish island-style. The portions are huge and the prices are good. This is a popular dining spot with the locals.

Competition for space is fierce. These yellow filter-feeding tube sponges have grown from this former star coral that has itself been overgrown by fire coral.

Golden Pagoda   949-5475

This fine Chinese restaurant is on West Bay Road. The daily lunch buffet features chicken, beef and spicy shrimp delights.

Lone Star Bar & Grill   945-5575

Owned by a dyed-in-the-saddle Texan, the Lone Star offers Tex-Mex food with a twice weekly special of all you can eat fajitas.

Rum Point Club Restaurant   947-9412

For a panoramic view of the North Sound in a relaxing, open-air atmosphere, try this spot. Marinated conch, Rum Point pepperpot or gazpacho soup are recommended starters. Test your palate with jerk pork kabob with sweet plantain and pineapple or order a black pepper tuna with tropical fruit salsa. To get there take the 40-minute ferry ride from the Hyatt dock.

Seaview   945-0058

Seaview offers good food, both island and continental, with nightly specials and a fresh salad bar.

Fresh fish is on the menus of most restaurants. Here, fishermen clean and weigh their catches as they've done for decades, while a modern cruise ship disembarks its passengers at George Town.

West Bay Polo Club   949-9892

The Polo Club features seafood, steaks and oriental specialties along with killer stir fries.

Whitehall Bay   949-8670

This casual patio restaurant serves stewed conch, turtle steak, crab backs, curried chicken, shrimp and lobster dishes.

Inexpensive

Chicken! Chicken!   945-2290

Spit-roasted chicken coated with a delicious combination of lemon juice, herbs (primarily rosemary) and other spices is the special here. Also served are great accompaniments such as tarragon carrots and pasta with pesto.

Eats—Crocodile Rock Cafe   945-5288

Fresh salads for lunch or dinner and the best blueberry pancakes on the island can all be had at bargain prices at Eats. The dinner menu is also quite good and reasonably priced.

Fast food. Most of the familiar fast food franchises are on Grand Cayman including: McDonald's, Burger King, Kentucky Fried Chicken, Wendy's, Subway and Pizza Hut. There's even Domino's Pizza delivery.

Night life. Grand Cayman has numerous night life attractions. For those who like to bar- and club-hop, there's plenty of action along Seven Mile Beach. Many places have live music, some have a local, Caribbean flavor and others feature a "top ten" selection.

Brightly colored Christmas tree worms extend their 2-inch-long (5 cm) spiraled gills from a tube fused to the base of a purple sea fan.

Guests at Cayman Brac's resorts create personalized sign posts for fun and posterity.

There's everything from calypso and country to live jazz and blues. The Seven Mile Beach strip also has two comedy clubs that have celebrity appearances on a regular basis. Two local theaters schedule stage dramas throughout the year.

Low key nighttime possibilities include going to the movies or simply taking a peaceful walk along a moonlit beach.

CAYMAN BRAC

Dining. Brac resorts have dining facilities for their guests, and all inclusive and partial food plans are available. Cayman Brac has several places to eat that serve local specials such as conch, island beef, pork, fish and lobster. Edd's Place is located at Tibbetts Square near the airport and serves local seafood and Chinese dishes. The nearby G & M Diner serves burgers, chicken and local food; Aunt Sha's and Sonja's are also on the West End and feature island menus. For a pizza or sub, try Angie's at Tibbetts Square. La Esperanza on the north shore, eight miles east of the airport, serves turtle stew, fresh fish and a local Caymanian dish called run-down; Blackie's Drive-In, also located east of Stake Bay on the north shore, has burgers and chicken. The Captain's Table is a new eatery located at the Brac Caribbean Villa condominiums, on the south side half-mile west of the cross-island road. Dinners include steaks, pasta primavera, and shrimp caribe; lunch selections include salads and burgers.

Night life. Night life on Cayman Brac is pretty much limited to the evening activities at the two resorts. Typical evening activities include slide shows, underwater videos and tapes of popular movies. Occasionally, local bands perform at one of the resorts. For guaranteed action on Saturday night, check out the live band and dancing at La Esperanza.

LITTLE CAYMAN

Dining. Like the Brac, Little Cayman resorts offer all inclusive meal plans. The island also has one small grocery store, and the recently completed restaurant and sports bar, the Hungry Iguana. The rental cottages and villas have fully-equipped kitchens.

For an adventure of the palate, visit Pirate's Point Resort, owned and operated by Gladys

Purple sea fans, a type of soft or gorgonian coral, thrive in Cayman's shallow reefs and along the tops of drop-offs. Look carefully among their branches for flamingo tongue snails.

Howard, a Cordon Bleu chef from Texas. Pirate's Point Resort was named one of the top 250 best restaurants in the world by Bon Appetit magazine. Meals at Pirate's Point are described as country cuisine and old fashioned Caymanian with fresh vegetables and fish.

Night life. Most who visit Little Cayman go there to get away from the bustle of mainstream tourist activities. The allures are peace, privacy and sensational diving. Nights are quiet and refreshing. After-dark things to do include walks on the beach, watching bioluminescence sparkle along the shoreline, or viewing the constellations and shooting stars overhead. Other possible night excitement are fishing and of course, scuba diving.

CHAPTER **V** DIVING

Caribbean Benchmark

Boat Diving

Most Cayman diving is done by boat. More than 40 operators on Grand Cayman run a virtual fleet of modern dive boats. Trips to the reefs or drop-offs are normally a 10- to 30-minute boat ride. For those who can't get enough on a two-tank dive, consider one of the all-day, three-tank boat trips offered by Sunset Divers and Parrot's Landing.

Conservation

The following activities are strictly prohibited:

- Taking of any marine life alive or dead including fishes, corals, sponges and shells. (Shells can be collected only on the beach.)
- Spearfishing with guns or poles.
- Damaging coral or other marine life.
- Fishing with gill nets or poisons. (Hook and line fishing is permitted in most areas.)
- Littering or dumping.
- Injuring or molesting turtles.
- Taking conch or lobster in Marine Park, Replenishment, or Environmental Zones.

Penalties for violations are severe and can cost up to $5,000 and a one-year jail sentence. Ask a Cayman operator for the pamphlet on conservation laws that gives a comprehensive listing of regulations and has a map of the various parks and zones.

Cayman operators discourage divers from wearing gloves, the justification being that divers are less likely to touch live coral with bare hands. It's a good idea to keep a pair of gloves in your BC pocket for use on hang stops or wrecks away from the reef.

The Cayman government has implemented a system of permanent moorings at the most frequently visited sites in Grand Cayman, Cayman Brac and Little Cayman. More than 225 of these moorings are currently maintained. The boat moorings protect the reefs from damage caused by anchors and swinging chains. The mooring program, in conjunction with a strongly promoted conservation awareness effort, is a result of the Cayman Marine Management System established in 1986 that divides the reef areas into three zones of concern: Marine Park, Replenishment and Environmental. Each zone has special regulations and restrictions. Most dive sites are in the marine park areas. The Cayman Marine Management Program has been used as a model by a number of other Caribbean islands.

Dive Operators

Most Cayman dive operators belong to the Cayman Islands Watersports Operators Association (CIWOA) which is at the forefront of diver safety, education and conservation issues. Most operations are well-equipped, modern facilities. Dive briefings typically include helpful information about the site as well as safety and marine conservation rules.

Grand Cayman. The majority of the Grand Cayman operators are located on the west end near Seven Mile Beach, but three are located on the far east end and one is in Bodden Town. Two others are situated on the north

Although sponges themselves are mostly undesirable as food, their cavities are often used by small fishes and shrimps as a haven from predators. These magnificent tube sponges are at Aquarium Reef.

Cayman's warm, calm, clear waters make entries as easy as taking a plunge in a swimming pool.

side. Most have at least two dive boats, but some of the larger operators have as many as seven boats.

The dive operations generally offer a two-tank morning dive that leaves between 8 and 10 A.M. Many also offer an afternoon dive that leaves between 1 and 2:30 P.M. Be sure to confirm dive schedules before you book rather than relying on possible outdated brochures or ads. Many of the afternoon boat dives are offered on a demand-only basis. Stingray City dives are usually made in the early afternoon, but some operators offer morning dives to Stingray City or Sandbar. Certain operators have a regular schedule for night dives, and others operate on a request-only basis.

Cayman Brac. Cayman Brac has two modern dive resorts, one independent operator, and is

home port to one liveaboard dive boat. All are conveniently located on the west end of the south shore, minutes from the airport.

The Tiara Beach Resort is part of the Divi Hotel and Resort chain which hosts the Peter Hughes Dive Tiara facility. The usual schedule includes a morning two-tank dive (wall and shallow) and an afternoon single-tank dive. Afternoon and night shore dives are offered as well as boat night dives. Depending on the weather, several two- and three-tank trips are made each week to Little Cayman's Bloody Bay Wall. The boat run to Little Cayman is 45 minutes.

Brac Aquatics operates on the south side at the Brac Caribbean Villa Condos. A morning two-tank dive leaves at 8:45 A.M. Afternoon shore and boat dives normally leave at 2:30

P.M. Night dives from shore are planned several times a week. Weather permitting, Brac Aquatics also makes at least two trips a week to Little Cayman.

Reef Divers at the Brac Reef Beach Resort offers boat diving, unlimited reef diving, and has a full service underwater photo and video center. Trips to Little Cayman are made two to three times a week.

Little Cayman. Until 1993, Pirate's Point, Sam McCoy's and Southern Cross were Little Cayman's only dive resorts—all small and pretty much self-contained. The fourth option was added when the Little Cayman Resort opened. The newest dive business is Paradise Divers, a full-service dive store and Little Cayman's first independent dive operator. All Little Cayman resorts and dive operators are within minutes of the famous Bloody Bay Wall and Jackson Point area on the north side. When the winds pick up from the north, boats head to the numerous moored sites on the south side.

DIVING REGULATIONS

Most dive operators belong to the Cayman Islands Watersport Operators Association (CIWOA), enforce a no deeper than 100 feet (30 m) rule and insist all divers return with 500 psi (34.5 bar) in their tanks. They also maintain a 1:10 guide/diver ratio for wall dives and always hang an emergency regulator at 10 feet (3 m). Most operators allow experienced divers to use computers. Stipulations are that each member of a buddy team must have their own dive computer, and bottom times can be extended no closer than five minutes to the no decompression limit. The maximum depth limit and the 500 psi (34.5 bar) return-air pressure rule also apply.

EQUIPMENT

Many dive operations have rental equipment and Grand Cayman has several full service dive stores that have retail sales as well as rental gear. Travelers headed to Cayman Brac or Little Cayman should always make arrangements for equipment rentals in advance.

SAFETY

The Cayman Island Watersports Operators Association (CIWOA) has safety as their utmost priority. The wall dives in Cayman are closely guided and the CIWOA regulations are firmly enforced. Dive safety, marine conservation and reef features are normally addressed in the pre-dive briefings. Lines and hang bars are positioned at 10 feet (3 m) after every dive for offgassing.

NIGHT DIVING

After sunset, coral reefs undergo a dramatic transformation. New shapes and colors appear, critters emerge, and the mood of the reef changes. Coral polyps extend for feeding, brittle stars decorate the vase sponges and red night shrimp light up the reef with their tiny reflective eyes. Colorful crinoids extend their arms to filter feed and basket stars make their debut in the darkness.

Larger critters like lobsters and crabs forage around the reef, and octopuses slide along the contours and through narrow fissures. Moray eels leave their lairs and swim freely through the reef. Sleepy parrotfishes can be seen in their transparent, mucus generated cocoons. Other reef fishes slow down to their nocturnal level of activity. Enjoy the night life, but be courteous about where you point your dive lights to avoid scaring these nighttime animals.

A two-man, double lock recompression chamber is located at the hospital in George Town (phone 555). The Cayman Island Divers, a branch of the British Sub-Aqua Club, maintains and operates the chamber with volunteers. One can never be too conservative, especially when making repetitive or deep dives. When diving the tables or computers, always add a safety margin to your no-decompression limit. Also, always ascend slowly and make a three- to five-minute safety stop at 10 to 15 feet (3-5 m) after every dive. Use the mooring line or the hang bar under the dive boat for your stop.

Remember to bring your C-card and log. Cayman operators will not allow scuba diving without proper verification.

SHORE DIVING

Cayman's many shore diving options appeal to both beginner and experienced divers. Dive buddies can set their own schedule and do their own thing with few restrictions. The safe, shallow close-in patch reefs provide excellent conditions for novices yet host enough critters to make the dives interesting. Some sites have caverns and tunnels, and others have ledges and mini-walls.

Grand Cayman. On Grand Cayman one can get in a lot of dives by renting a car, picking up gear and driving to a number of shore entries for reef, wreck and even wall dives. There's also several operators with shoreside facilities that cater to shore divers. Popular facilities close to George Town include Parrot's Landing, Bob Soto's, Eden Rock Dive Centre, Sunset Divers and Divetech. These operators rent tanks and weights, and the dive staffs assist in check-out and orientation.

The West Wall can be reached from several shore points south of George Town, but the swim out is a good 100 to 150 yards (91-136 m).

Cayman Brac. The shore dive sites on Cayman Brac are on the north side of the island which is the side opposite the resorts. Trucks are used to shuttle divers and

In this birds-eye view of the northeast shore of Grand Cayman, the spur and groove formations, which are parallel ridges of coral interspersed with sand patches, are clearly visible. The white mooring ball on lower right is at a remote dive site called Babylon.

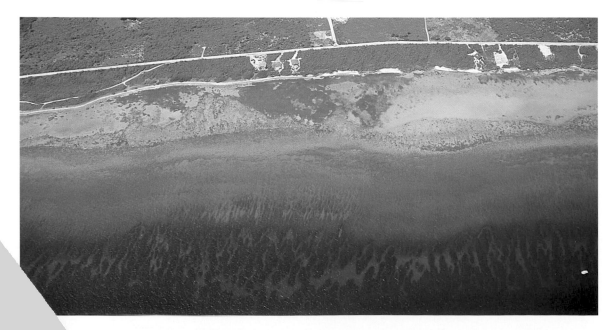

With clear, calm water and easy shore access, the Caymans are ideal for resort scuba courses where the basic skills are taught, and a reef dive is made all in the same day.

equipment to the entry points. The shallow spur and groove reef formations are typically dived on afternoons and at night.

Little Cayman. The best entry points for shore dives on Little Cayman are near Jackson Point on the north side. Shore dives with easy access just west of Jackson Point include Cumber's Caves, Bus Stop, Sarah's Set and Salt Rocks.

TOPOGRAPHY

The Cayman Islands are actually three mountain tops along an undersea ridge that runs between Cuba and Honduras. The surrounding waters are thousands of feet deep; the famous Cayman Trench east of the Caymans bottoms out at 24,000 feet (7.273 m). Each island is rimmed with a shallow shelf of lush coral reefs. These flat, limestone islands have no rivers or runoff to cloud the shoreline waters with sediment. As a result, Cayman waters are crystal clear year-round.

The Caymans have a diversity of coral formations that provides endless opportunities for exploration, however, there are some general similarities to the layout of the reefs. Small coral heads or shallow fringing reefs comprised of mostly stony corals—brain, star and staghorn—begin immediately from the shore. Depths vary from 10 to 30 feet (3-9 m). Areas preceding and between the patches of corals are generally flat and sandy. Farther from shore the bottom slopes more steeply and the coral clusters increase in size, forming elongated sections of spurs separated by narrow strips of sand, known simply as "spur-and-groove" formations. The bottom slopes

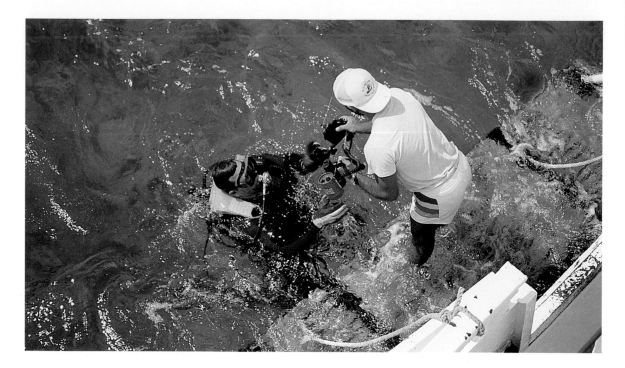

For underwater photographers of all levels, the clear water and abundant marine life make the Caymans an ideal destination. Photo instruction is readily available.

Dive boats are modern and well equipped in the Caymans. Some even have extra deckhands such as this iguana, a harmless reptile that prefers the sunny deck to the water.

even greater to a depth of about 40 to 60 feet (12-18 m) where a sloping drop-off or wall is formed. Some of the drop-offs are gradual; others are sheer or even undercut. Many of the walls are riddled with tunnels, chimneys and archways.

TRAINING AND EXPERIENCE LEVELS

Cayman operators are equipped to accommodate divers from novice to highly experienced. Besides full certification programs, most operators offer a "resort course" which includes two hours of pool training in scuba gear along with instruction in essential aspects of diving physiology and physics. This is followed by a 30-minute open water dive under close supervision.

A full certification course involves hours of class work and pool exercises. In addition, some operators offer advanced programs.

After a number of dives where essential scuba skills are demonstrated, especially a proficiency in buoyancy control, divers are permitted to dive with their buddies unguided. Instead of being constrained to the group's pre-set maximum bottom time, buddy teams can dive with their computers and are allowed more latitude to explore the walls and reefs on their own.

UNDERWATER PHOTOGRAPHY

The Caymans are ideal for underwater photography. The calm, clear conditions, abundance of friendly, colorful subjects, and access to professionals for tips and guidance are all the ingredients needed for achieving excellent results. If you need to rent a camera, strobe or underwater video, it's no problem. More than a dozen Cayman operators rent an array of camera and video equipment, and there are several full service photo centers that offer photo courses. The in-water guidance and same-day critique of your work enable a fast learning process. If you bring your own equipment, it's nice to know that when "Murphy" strikes, expert support is nearby.

VISIBILITY

Visibility in the Caymans is a benchmark for the Western Hemisphere. Average visibility is 100 feet (30 m), but on a great day it can exceed 200 feet (61 m).

WATER TEMPERATURE

The water temperature varies from a low of 78 to 80°F (26-27°C) in the winter to a constant 85°F (29°C) throughout the summer. An eighth-inch (3 mm) wet suit or shortie is suggested for winter diving. In the summer a lycra suit is all that's needed unless you chill easily.

A feather duster extends its soft plumed gills to snare plankton floating with the current.

CHAPTER **VI**   GRAND CAYMAN SITES

Grand Cayman is encircled by a constellation of exciting dive sites that vary from fish-filled shallows to breathtaking walls. Wall diving is the definite trademark of the Cayman Islands; there are more than 100 named drop-offs around the main island alone.

NORTH WALL AND NORTH SOUND

Grand Cayman's North Wall is dived far less than the West Wall or the southwest side. The north is the windward side of the island which means conditions are not as good during the winter months. When you do get to dive the North Wall, you'll find the formations awesome. In some places the undersea cliffs are sheer and in others they are sharply undercut. Bathed in air-clear water, and profuse with sponges and corals of every imaginable hue, many consider Grand Cayman's North Wall an experience close or equal to the legendary Bloody Bay Wall at Little Cayman.

1. GHOST MOUNTAIN

DEPTH:	70-100+ FEET
	(21-30+ M)

Ghost Mountain is located just off Grand Cayman's North Point. The "mountain" is an enormous mushroom-shaped undersea pinnacle jutting off the main wall. The base of the formation meets the sloping wall at a depth of more than 100 feet (30 m) with the top of the pinnacle at 70 feet (21 m). Ghost Mountain is loaded with schooling fishes that include hundreds of swirling horse-eye jacks. These fast-moving, silvery fish swim in unison and often make close sweeps between divers.

Hordes of creole wrasse are plentiful over

the reef and the pinnacle is covered with brown and yellow tube sponges, lavender and bright-red finger sponges, and spires of starlet corals. You'll see an opening to a cave near the pinnacle base at a depth of 120 feet (36 m), but don't try entering it because it's below the maximum allowable depth.

2. STINGRAY CITY (S)

DEPTH:	12-15 FEET
	(4-5 M)

Stingray City is located in the North Sound just inshore from Tarpon Alley. This area consists mostly of shallow sand flats 12 to 15 feet (4-5 m) deep, spotted with small coral heads. The 30 or more southern stingrays that inhabit this site perform an action-packed feeding display that provides non-stop fun and entertainment. Stingray City is also home for Bruce, a friendly 6-foot (2 m) green moray eel that is hand fed regularly by divemasters.

Upon entering the water, divers and snorkelers are immediately greeted by a squadron of hungry, but gentle southern stingrays. Most are females whose disk-shaped bodies are 3 to 4 feet (1-1.2 m) across. The few males that hang around are noticeably smaller and have claspers at the base of their tails.

Pay close attention to the dive guide before attempting to feed one. It's not so much the rays and their powerful grinding plates as it is the voracious yellowtail snapper that often

Blue tangs normally graze on algae, but they are also known to compete with the rays and the voracious yellowtail snapper for handouts at Stingray City.

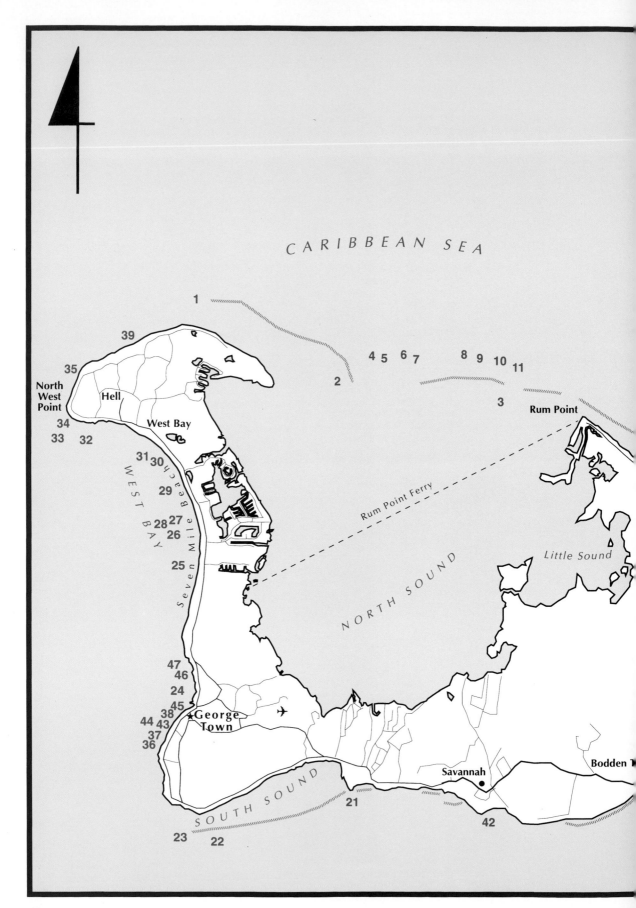

CARIBBEAN SEA

1

39

35

North
West
Point

Hell

West Bay

34

33   32

31 30

29

28 27
26

25

WEST BAY

Seven Mile Beach

47
46

24

45
38
44 43
37
36

George
Town

4 5   6 7   8 9   10   11

2

3

Rum Point

Rum Point Ferry

NORTH SOUND

Little Sound

SOUTH SOUND

21

23

22

Savannah

42

Bodden

GRAND CAYMAN

NORTH WALL & NORTH SOUND
1. Ghost Mountain
2. Stingray City
3. Sandbar
4. Tarpon Alley
5. Princess Penny Pinnacles
6. Eagle Ray Pass
7. Lemon Drop-off
8. Leslie's Curl
9. 3-B's Wall
10. Chinese Wall
11. Gale's Mountain

EAST
12. Babylon
13. Snapper Hole
14. Old Wreck Head
15. Grouper Grotto
16. Scuba Bowl
17. The Maze

18. Three Sisters
19. High Rock Drop-off
20. Ironshore Garden

SOUTH
21. Japanese Gardens
22. Kent's Caves
23. Big Table Rock

WEST
24. *Balboa*
25. Mesa
26. *Oro Verde*
27. Aquarium Reef
28. Eagle's Nest
29. Spanish Anchor
30. *Doc Polson*
31. Trinity Caves
32. Big Tunnel

33. Orange Canyon
34. Bonnie's Arch

SHORE DIVING
35. Turtle Farm Reef
36. Waldo's Reef
37. Sunset Reef
38. Devil's Grotto

ADDITIONAL SHORE SITES
39. Spanish Bay Reef
40. North Side
41. Babylon Mooring
42. Pedro's Castle
43. Parrot's Reef
44. Polly's Perch
45. Eden Rock
46. *Cali*
47. Soto's Reef

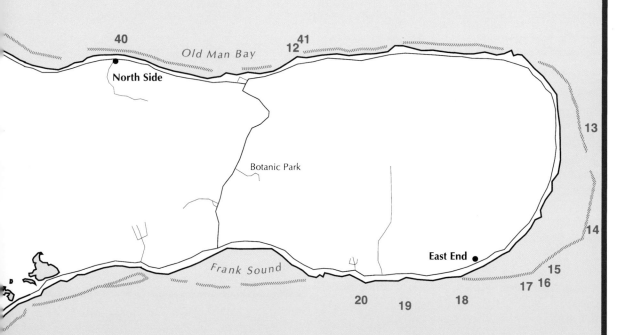

Stingray City, a mere 12 feet (3.6 m) deep, provides non-stop hours of fun for divers and snorkelers.

misjudge fingers for food. Keep your hand covering the bait at all times, and when the ray is within reach, feed it like you would sugar to a horse. Ballyhoo, a small beaked baitfish, is one of their favorite foods.

The sand bottom stirs easily, so it's best to plant yourself in one spot and take cues from the guide. The rays know if you have food. Even if they can't see it, they can smell it. The rays will politely bump you and rub against you in pursuit of a handout. When food is around, the rays are determined, but certainly pose no threat. As they pass by, gently stroke their bodies. Unlike their shark cousins, southern rays have smooth, velvety-soft skin. (Operators strictly enforce the "no gloves" rule at this site). Neither the human contact nor the scuba seem to bother the rays at all. Their 6-inch-long (15 cm) venomous and potentially dangerous spines remain relaxed against their tails.

Photography. The non-stop action at Stingray City, Sandbar and other stingray sites provides incredible potential for video and still photos. Backscatter can be a problem for strobe users, so be sure to shoot plenty of wide-angle, available light shots. At these shallow depths there is good light and colors.

The crowds, tour boats and hype aside, Stingray City remains a must dive when in the Caymans.

3. SANDBAR (S)

DEPTH:	3-10 FEET
	(1-3 M)

Sandbar is another stingray site located east of Stingray City just inside the Rum Point Channel. The shallow depth at Sandbar is ideal for snorkelers, but many prefer scuba to maximize bottom time with the friendly rays.

You can expect the same experience here as at Stingray City (see Site 2). Look for an all-black ray at this site. His nickname is Darth Vader.

Feeding the Cayman rays is an unforgettable marine life encounter and is one of those few single dives that can highlight an entire vacation.

Stingray Alley, another North Sound stingray site like the others, features a parade of friendly southern rays at a shallow, sandy site.

4. TARPON ALLEY

DEPTH:	50-80 FEET
	(15-24 M)

Tarpon are seen on a regular basis at more than a dozen Grand Cayman sites. Some sites have 10 to 20 permanent residents, but at Tarpon Alley near the North Sound, at least a hundred of these silver kings find food and refuge in the reef. Most are 2^1/$_2$ to 3 feet (76-92 cm) long but some reach 4 feet (1.2 m) in length. The tarpon school inside a long, narrow canyon cut in the reef close to the drop-off. Swim slow and steady to get a close look at these magnificent fish. You'll notice their huge, shiny scales, long dorsal filaments and bulldog mouths.

Southern stingrays, barracuda, yellowtail snappers, porkfish and small schools of sennet are also common at this site. Sennet are long, silvery fish that are smaller and even more slender than their cousin, the barracuda. This is always a good spot to see hawksbill turtles, so keep your eyes pealed.

Although this orange encrusting sponge has transparent cavities that appear delicate and soft, they thrive on star coral colonies and can be irritating to touch.

5. PRINCESS PENNY PINNACLES

DEPTH:	45-100+ FEET
	(14-30+ M)

Located just west of Tarpon Alley, this site is named after Penny Ventura, a record holding free-diver. A plaque near the mooring pin has a poem inscribed in memory of her.

Heading toward the wall you'll see a large pinnacle, a series of coral buttresses, and at least two swim-through chimneys. The buttress just east of the mooring is lush with rope sponges, black corals and gorgonians. Look for brittle stars and coral shrimp in and around the large basket sponges.

Swim about 30 feet (9 m) west of the mooring to enter a chimney near the lip of the wall that exits the face at a depth of 80 feet (24 m). From there, swim east at a 90-foot depth (27 m) to find a second chimney that angles up and exits the reef at 45 feet (14 m). When entering this smaller cavern, you'll need to swim in a single file.

Reef sharks and spotted eagle rays frequently cruise this stretch of the North Wall.

The French angelfish, identified by its golden scales, is one of the most approachable of the angelfishes found in the Caymans.

6. EAGLE RAY PASS

DEPTH:	40-100 FEET
	(12-30 M)

Eagle Ray Pass, located straight out from the North Sound's Main Channel, features a canyon approach to a massive coral archway that cuts through the wall and fans out to form a wide sandy slope. As the name implies, this is a great site for encountering eagle rays. Spotted eagle rays are easily identified by their exceptionally long, whip-like tails and leopard-spotted body. Don't be too surprised if you even encounter a blacktip shark or a scalloped hammerhead cruising along the wall.

Eagle Ray Pass is also a good second dive since the top of the wall is only 40 feet (12 m) deep. You can fin along the wall down to 60 feet (18 m) or explore the shallow reefs south of the mooring. Look for spiny lobsters under the coral ledges. You can often spot their moving antennae sticking out of crevices between the ledges.

7. LEMON DROP-OFF

DEPTH:	50-100+ FEET
	(15-30+ M)

This site is located northeast of the North Sound's Main Channel and features a series of parallel sand gullies that spill over the rim of this relatively steep section of the North Wall. The mooring pin is within 20 feet (6 m) of the drop-off. The face of the wall is decorated with green finger sponges, tan sea rods, yellow tunicates and blue sea fans.

The reef above the wall is a favorite second dive. Action includes large green morays, not-so-bashful spiny lobsters and on occasion, green turtles. Harlequin bass—yellow bodied with dark tiger bars—drift above the bottom near a schoolmaster or two while an occasional solitary red hind sits still on the sand. Look for groups of yellowhead jawfish above their burrows in the sand flats.

8. LESLIE'S CURL

DEPTH:	55-100+ FEET
	(17-30+ M)

Leslie's Curl is a section of the North Wall between Eagle Ray Pass and Grand Canyon. The wall is actually undercut ("curls" under) and the shadowed reef area provides an ideal base for yellow tube tunicates. Dozens of these gelatinous filter-feeders thrive in the shadows at depths of 70 to 100 feet (21-30 m) directly seaward from the mooring. As is typical with this section of North Wall, deep ravines and fissures cut through the face of the wall. The sloping sections of the wall have terraces of flattened star corals, and the numerous sponge varieties on the face include mottled blue and yellow tubes, green finger and strawberry cups. You'll also see huge boulders of brain and star corals fused to the reef.

Schooling creole wrasse occupy the water column above the reef and bunches of black durgons feed closer to the coral. Look for green morays and spiny lobsters hiding in the shallow reef areas to the south.

9. 3-B'S WALL

DEPTH:	50-100+ FEET
	(15-30+ M)

The site known as 3-B's Wall is a breathtaking, undersea canyon that also goes by the name Grand Canyon. At this section of the North Wall, a wide recess is formed by two massive coral buttresses spaced over 100 feet (30 m) apart. The sides are sheer and blanketed with numerous sponge varieties strewn along with bushy colonies of soft corals. Visibility is usually more than 100 feet (30 m) and the view of this expansive formation is awesome.

Tiger grouper, Nassau grouper, rock beauties and gray angelfish are a few of the tropicals you're sure to see here. Schooling fishes include blue runners, gray Bermuda chub and purple creole wrasse. This is also a great wall dive for spotting pelagic cruisers such as green turtles and the majestic spotted eagle rays.

Snorkeling (S)

The Cayman Islands have ideal conditions for snorkeling. The shoreline waters are warm, clear and calm year-round, and the shallow patch reefs close to shore abound with colorful and interesting marine life. Most snorkeling is done right from the beach or ironshore, but there's also the option of reserving a boat ride to any of a number of exciting shallow reefs. Many of the popular Grand Cayman shore snorkeling spots are off the Northwest Point, near George Town and along the South Sound area. The dive sites described in this book are marked with an (S) if they are good for snorkeling.

Spanish Bay Reef, Hepp's Pipeline and Bonnie's Arch are excellent sites north of Seven Mile Beach; Devil's Grotto, Eden Rock and Parrot's Reef are easily accessed from Parrot's Landing or the Eden Rock Dive Center. Waldo's Reef is a bit farther south. Other frequented shore sites include Soto's Reef, Fishpot Reef, Seaview Reef, the shipwreck *Cali* and the wreck of the *Balboa*, a 375-foot-long (114 m) freighter that sunk in George Town harbor 60 years ago. Spot's Reef, just east of Japanese Gardens, is a great spot on the south side. Some of the sites that require boat access are Aquarium Reef, Mesa, and the shipwreck *Oro Verde*—all off of Seven Mile Beach. There's also good snorkeling off of Rum Point and several spots on the East End including the wreck of the *Ridgefield*.

Snorkeling is done off both the north and south shores of Cayman Brac, but there's definitely better reef access on the north side. Little Cayman snorkel sites include Pirate's Point Reef, the reef near Salt Rocks and the stretch of Jackson Bay between Picnic Grounds and Bus Stop.

The most popular snorkeling site in the Caymans or the entire world for that matter, is Stingray City in Grand Cayman's North Sound. Most Cayman operators accommodate snorkelers and several specialize in snorkel cruises. Snorkeling gear is available for rent throughout the islands.

10. CHINESE WALL

DEPTH:	50-100+ FEET
	(15-30+ M)

At Chinese Wall, head north from the mooring pin set at a depth of 50 feet (15 m) to find a deep ravine leading to the wall. The fissure cuts between two protruding masses of coral.

Both coral buttresses are blanketed with purple sea whips, sea rods and numerous varieties of stony corals. Iridescent vase sponges, strawberry sponges and yellow tube sponges add to the array of colorful animal life on the face of the wall.

A deep pocket of sand east of the mooring has scattered coral heads and small schools of snapper along with a red hind or two. Green and hawksbill turtles often pass along the reef-top.

11. GALE'S MOUNTAIN

DEPTH:	50-100+ FEET
	(15-30+ M)

This unusual undersea mount rises to within 50 feet (15 m) of the surface just north of Rum Point. At a depth of 75 feet (23 m), you'll see a deep ravine cut around the perimeter, separating the peak from the base section. There are a number of other smaller fissures and canyons, including a long straight run on the north side that cuts down the slope. Clouds of blue chromis, purple creole wrasse and other small fishes hover above the coral heads feeding on plankton. An occasional glance away from the wall toward the open blue could reward you with a sight of schooling jacks or spotted eagle rays.

EAST END

The East End and eastern sections of the North and South Walls are the least dived on the island. Only four dive operators, a live-aboard dive boat, and a couple of all-day boats leaving from the west end of the island have access to the eastern reefs. The East End has more than 60 named dives and less than half have moorings. The 25-mile (40 km) long horseshoe-shaped stretch of walls from Rum Point to the far East End and back along the south side to Bodden Town are as pristine today as they were 50 years ago.

On night dives you'll discover the colorful and interesting critters, like this star-eyed hermit crab that spends the day in inconspicuous hide-outs.

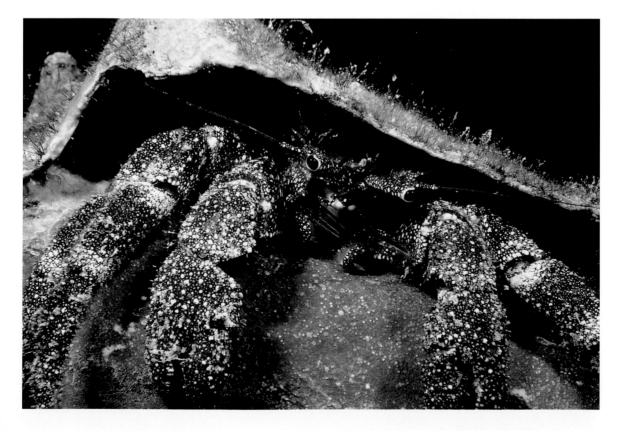

This aerial view of the East End of Grand Cayman shows the reef line at the Morritt's Tortuga Club. The East End is one of the least dived areas in the Caymans.

12. BABYLON

DEPTH:	40-100+ FEET
	(12-30+ M)

Babylon is a dramatic undersea formation about midway between Morritt's Tortuga Club and Rum Point. The lip of the wall is at 40 feet (12 m). The face angles to a depth of just over 100 feet (30 m) where it meets the base of a huge pillar not far off the main wall. The deep-water gorgonians, sponges and black coral bushes between the wall and the pinnacle are so thick that it takes a careful look to find a clear passageway. The massive pinnacle is at least 70 feet (21 m) across, and is blanketed with corals and sponges as well as giant pink-tipped anemones. Look closely in the anemones for the tiny diamond blennies. The outer side of the pinnacle rises to a depth of 40 feet (12 m) which is the same depth as the main wall.

Pelagic life cruising this section of the North Wall include spotted eagle rays, green turtles and bull sharks.

Babylon can be accessed from shore, but it's a long swim and should be attempted only by highly experienced divers under ideal surface conditions.

During the day longjaw squirrelfish are often seen under ledges or near crevices in the reef. Their large eyes make them especially adapted to hunting at night, and as dusk approaches they will become increasingly active.

Nudibranchs are mollusks in the same phylum as clams and octopuses. The banana nudibranch shown here feeds mainly at night on algae and is particularly fond of feeding on bushy sea whips.

13. SNAPPER HOLE

DEPTH:	65 FEET
	(20 M)

Snapper Hole consists of an incredible network of chutes, cuts, tunnels and caverns. Along with pristine formations of star and brain corals, you will see a stately spire of pillar coral. Schools of snapper congregate near the ledges and Bermuda chub work the water column above the reef. Silversides and at least 60 tarpon occupy many of the caverns and tunnels. Other large animals you are likely to encounter include blacktip sharks, eagle rays and nurse sharks. A signature of this site is the sponge-encrusted anchor from the wreck of the *Methusalem*, a 300-foot-long (91 m) tanker now broken into scattered pieces. The anchor stands upright in a sand hole and is positioned well for use as a photo prop.

14. OLD WRECK HEAD (S)

DEPTH:	50 FEET
	(15 M)

Old Wreck Head is a site located just outside

During the day, parrotfishes patrol the reef while munching on coral with their fused teeth to extract the algae. At night they enter a sleep-like state of turpor, often enshrouded in a cocoon of mucus which is believed to hide their scent from predators. Be careful not to disturb or intrude while they sleep.

the East End's east channel, an area renowned for shipwrecks. You'll see several sections of rusted wreckage jutting out of the water. Old Wreck Head, formerly known as Shark Alley, has a series of coral ridges and a network of caverns filled with 3-foot-long (1 m) tarpon. There must be 50 at this site alone. Tarpon can be a little skittish, but here they allow you to get very close—face to face! Head east of the mooring to find the largest congregation in a large cavern having a 12-foot by 12-foot (4 m by 4 m) opening.

As you pass through the caves, you'll also find several species of squirrelfish and snapper. Graysby, yellow coneys and goatfish feed around the reef outside the caverns. Look for yellowhead jawfish hovering above their tiny

sand burrows, tilefish pulsating above their larger burrows, and scorpionfish hiding at the edge of the reef.

15. GROUPER GROTTO (S)

DEPTH:	20-50 FEET
	(6-15 M)

The mooring at Grouper Grotto is on a tabletop of coral 20 feet (6 m) deep. The shallows, also excellent for snorkeling, have scattered brain corals, gorgonian whips, small stands of elkhorn coral and gold sea fans. Huge schools of Bermuda chub feed near the surface

Christmas tree tube worms and an encrusting sponge compete for space between polyps of a star coral. At the first sign of danger, often a shadow or water movement caused by a diver, the worm will quickly retract its gill whorl, locking itself behind a trap door. If you are patient the whorl may slowly re-emerge.

while schoolmasters and other reef fishes work the top of the reef.

There is a ledge at the edge of the flat reeftop where the depth drops to 50 feet (23 m). The deeper topography consists of a series of canyons, ravines and archways which is very characteristic of this side of the island. Don't expect to find groupers in the grottos. Instead, dozens of large, silvery tarpon bide their time in the coral canyons. From August through September, the patient tarpon get to feast on the large schools of silversides that fill the canyons.

Spotted eagle rays make regular passes through the sand alleyways east of the mooring.

16. SCUBA BOWL

DEPTH:	65-100+ FEET
	(20-30+ M)

This site, located just outside the East End's south channel, is where the edge of the wall winds continuously in and out in a zigzag fashion. The depth at the top of the wall also varies considerably—from 65 to 80 feet (18-23 m) deep. Deep ravines and gorges cut through the face of the wall. You'll see boulder-sized brain corals, huge chandelier gorgonians, large blue fan corals and lavender finger sponges at this site. Look for trumpetfish mimicking the finger sponges or trying to hide behind deep-water gorgonians.

A dense garden of feathery soft corals fill the top of the wall. Mutton and dog snappers, which are active nocturnal feeders, hang out or swim slowly through the reef during the day. Blacktips and silvery Caribbean reef sharks show up at this site from time to time.

17. THE MAZE

DEPTH:	55-100+ FEET
	(17-30+ M)

The Maze, an East End anchor dive, is situated between Three Sisters and Scuba Bowl. This site features a labyrinth of deep, narrow coral ravines that forms, as the name implies, a convolution of passageways. Operators normally drop anchor in a sand canyon that is about 75 feet (23 m) deep. As you swim (due

south) following the main ravine toward the drop-off, you'll notice that it ends in a large recessed section of the wall that has two huge coral pinnacles. If you swim outside the wall to the east, you'll find another smaller pinnacle. All three pinnacles are loaded with sponges and soft corals. The main wall is also decorated with a long list of colorful fauna and trees of black coral. This site is a good bet for spotting green turtles, spotted eagle rays and Caribbean reef sharks.

18. THREE SISTERS

DEPTH:	55-100+ FEET
	(17-30+ M)

The "three sisters" at this East End site are named Agnes, Bertha and Claire. The names refer to three mammoth coral pinnacles that prominently protrude from the main wall. The

Star coral polyps extend their tentacles at night to snare plankton in the passing currents.

Juvenile French angelfish are often found fluttering busily around the reef near holes and crevices.

At night, almost wherever you shine your dive light on the reef, the highly reflective eyes of shrimps glow back like tiny fireflies.

Peacock flounders are experts of camouflage. They are hard to spot with their distinctive patterns, and they often bury themselves in the sand so well that they often go unnoticed.

Green moray eels, like this one encountered at High Rock Drop-off, occasionally emerge from their lairs to swim freely across the reef.

bases of the three formations begin at depths well below 100 feet (30 m) and rise to within 60 feet (18 m) of the surface. A thick mass of multi-hued sponges, soft gorgonians and stony corals cover the giant spires. The main wall sports giant gorgonian fans and bushes of black coral. Look for spotted eagle rays gliding along the wall.

19. HIGH ROCK DROP-OFF

DEPTH:	45-100+ FEET
	(14-30+ M)

Situated just west of Three Sisters, High Rock

Tube sponges, red finger sponges and gorgonian corals accent the breathtaking wall at the East End's High Rock Drop-off.

Drop-off is named for its location offshore from an area called High Rocks. Large feathery coral sea plumes, sea rods and sea whips cover the top of the wall. Just east of the mooring, the wall has a noticeable bulge. Two large coral pinnacles jut off the wall on either side of the hump. Both pinnacles are lush with corals and top off at 60 feet (18 m).

Swimming along the upper wall, you'll see large mounds of brain and mountainous star corals along with deep-water gorgonians. Princess and queen parrotfish graze on the algae in and around the corals as schools of black durgons, a shy type of triggerfish, roam the reeftop. Schools of yellowtail snapper with their yellow stripe and forked tails are abundant at this site.

Scorpionfish have venomous spines and are difficult to spot because they are masters of camouflage. To avoid a painful surprise, practice proper bouyancy control and don't touch the reef or sea floor.

20. IRONSHORE GARDEN

DEPTH:	50 FEET
	(15 M)

This shallow East End site has a number of caves, tunnels, and winding coral canyons to explore. The coral gardens are enhanced by a thick cluster of brown elkhorn stands.

Ironshore Gardens is one of the East End's many tarpon dives. Dozens of these stately, chrome-plated fish school at this site, usually hovering or moving very slowly. Swim calmly and carefully to get a close-up look. As you approach them, tarpon will slowly disperse and after you swim through, they usually return to their original group formations.

SOUTH

In recent years the western end of Grand Cayman's South Wall is being visited increasingly by the Seven Mile Beach operators, especially during the winter months when the wind shifts to the northwest. Still this stretch of Cayman reef and drop-offs sees far fewer divers than the West Wall.

The South Wall generally starts a little deeper, and the shallow inside reef areas have coral grottos, mazes of sand alleyways, and gorgeous formations of elkhorn and staghorn corals which are absent on the north side.

The stately pillar coral, unlike most other corals, extends its polyps to feed during the day.

The tube of the red fan worm is usually seen embedded in star, lettuce and finger corals. Tiny bits of plankton and organic matter are filtered from the water by the worm's gills which also act like a strainer.

Southern stingrays are commonly seen in sand patches where they sometimes cover themselves with sand.

21. JAPANESE GARDENS (S)

DEPTH:	30-50 FEET
	(9-15 M)

Japanese Gardens is a wonderful second dive located inside the South Wall drop-off. Like Kent's Caves, this dive is noted for its conspicuous stands of elkhorn corals and large schools of Bermuda chub. Look for tiny, bright blue juvenile fish hiding out in the elkhorn branches.

There is a maze of passageways to explore and the fish-watching is excellent at this reef. Look up in the water column to see blue and brown chromis feeding on plankton; swim near the bottom in the shallow sand and rubble areas to find the burrowing yellowhead jawfish.

22. KENT'S CAVES (S)

DEPTH:	30-50 FEET
	(9-15 M)

Kent's Caves is a shallow site inside the South Wall drop-off that is characterized by a labyrinth of shallow caves and stands of golden elkhorn corals. Be sure to swim carefully around the elkhorn formations as they are easily damaged and can take decades to recover. This site has two moorings, one on the east side and a second on the west.

You may see green turtles swimming around the alleyways and you're likely to see a school of silvery tarpon near the caves. Nurse sharks are sometimes spotted at a large cave near the east mooring. Nassau grouper, bigeyes and schools of snapper are always seen at this site.

Caribbean basket stars, which are extremely sensitive to light, curl up into balls during the day. At night they emerge from their hiding places and extend their long arms to collect plankton.

23. BIG TABLE ROCK

DEPTH:	60-100+ FEET
	(18-30+ M)
CURRENT:	CAN BE VERY
	STRONG

Big Table Rock, an anchor dive on the far west end of South Sound, is about 30 minutes by boat from Parrot's Landing. The sloping wall starts at 60 feet (18 m) and the reef top features cuts and crevices with sand alleys that angle down toward the drop-off. This site is the original "Tarpon Alley" and you'll see tarpon here on every dive. You'll also see schools of barracuda on most dives and often encounter small blacktip sharks. Barracudas have the curiosity of a cat and like to approach and follow divers. When you confront a barracuda, it normally backs off and will often swim away. Blacktip sharks, on the other hand, are continuous fast movers and are generally very skittish around scuba divers.

WEST

The West Wall is Grand Cayman's most accessible and is dived with greatest frequency. There are more than 25 dive operators close by this 10-mile (16 km) stretch of reef and sloping drop-offs. There's no doubt this area shows some signs of "fin damage", yet the shallow sites inside the West Wall remain full of fishes, and are adorned with sponges and other colorful growth. At least 50 different sites have been named along the western stretch alone.

24. *BALBOA* (S)

DEPTH:	20-40 FEET
	(6-12 M)

The wreck of the *Balboa*, located 200 yards (183 m) off the George Town pier, is a good second dive and an outstanding night dive. Because of its location in a ship traffic lane, permission for diving is required from the

ADVANCED DIVING

Experienced, active and well-traveled divers deserve more freedom on their dives than do recently certified or occasional divers. Cayman dive operators recognize this and have instituted special programs to accommodate advanced divers.
Ambassador Divers, Bob Soto's, Divetech, Fisheye, Parrot's Landing, Sunset Divers and several other operators facilitate unguided, computer diving for buddy teams that have adequate experience and can demonstrate good diving skills, especially buoyancy control. On day and night dives, repeat divers who know the sites can decide for themselves where to spend their precious bottom time.

Unguided doesn't mean turned loose with no instructions. All divers are well-briefed regarding sites, conditions, safety and marine conservation. Only no-decompression dives are allowed, and no dives are permitted below 100 feet (30 m).

Long-spined sea urchins are active at night as they move along the reef grazing on algae.

harbormaster.

The *Balboa* was a 375-foot-long (99 m) freighter sunk in a 1932 hurricane. The hull is overturned and was dynamited into several pieces that now lay in an arc running east to west. Amid the twisted and strewn steel wreckage is a section of the boiler room, a large stern piece and the propeller. Action at night includes tiny bright red shrimp, octopuses, flaming scallops, sleeping parrotfishes and rare orange ball anemones.

25. MESA (S)

DEPTH:	30-50 FEET
	(9-15 M)

Mesa, also known as both Rhapsody and Fish Reef, is a small coral formation with a flat table-topped shape and vertical sides not unlike an underwater plateau or mesa. Located south of the *Oro Verde*, Mesa is a strong

magnet for reef fishes and also hosts an abundance of small invertebrates. There may be more fishes on this reef per square foot than any reef in the Caymans.

Mesa is an excellent choice for a second dive or a night dive. After dark, look for spiny lobsters, sleeping parrotfishes and red night shrimp. Expect to encounter very friendly French and gray angelfishes at this site.

26. ORO VERDE (S)

DEPTH:	55 FEET
	(17 M)

The 200-foot-long (61 m) *Oro Verde* is the first lady of Cayman shipwrecks. She was intentionally sunk in 1980 and now rests in 55 feet (17 m) of water directly off the Holiday Inn on Seven Mile Beach. Although battered and torn apart by Hurricane Gilbert and other storms, she remains a haven for an incredible

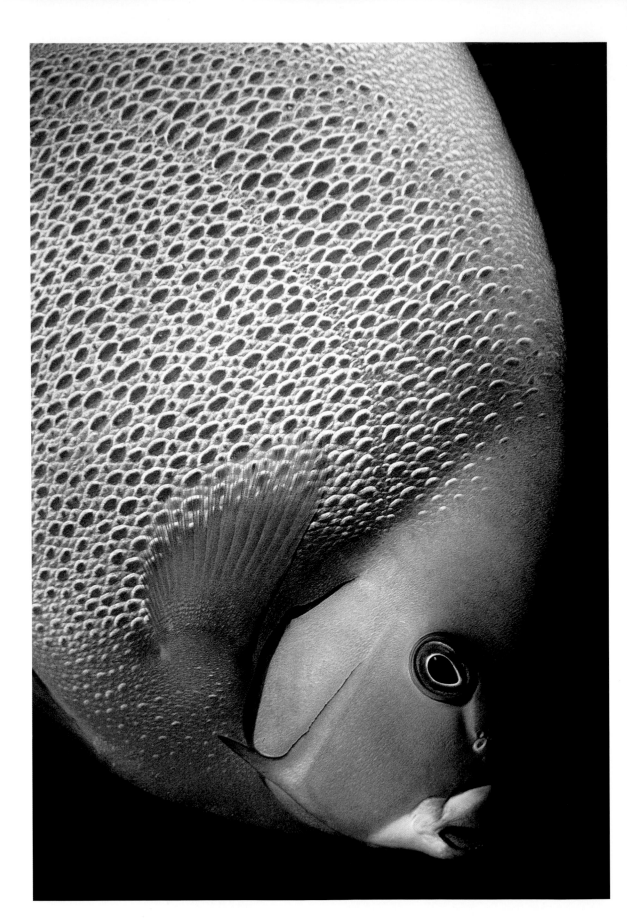

variety of tame marine life.

Need a close-up shot of a Nassau grouper named Wanda, a golden coney, a toothy barracuda or a green moray? No problem at this site. Just be ready to rack your lens to minimum focus. Not to be overlooked are the nearby sand flats that host shy garden eels, resting southern stingrays and cagey lizardfish.

27. AQUARIUM REEF

DEPTH:	50 FEET
	(15 M)

This site is renowned for its very friendly fishes. The resident snappers, groupers and sergeant majors are somewhat aggressive, and even the gray and French angelfishes beg for diver handouts. Because of its shallow depth, Aquarium Reef is a popular night dive and a favorite second dive during the day. Spiny lobsters hide under the many ledges and several large groupers are regulars at this reef. A prominent stand of a light tan pillar coral is within sight of the mooring; their tall fuzzy spires are unmistakable. Also, there's a special overhang at this site where lobsters and even nurse sharks sometimes take refuge.

28. EAGLE'S NEST

DEPTH:	50-100 FEET
	(15-30 M)

Eagle's Nest is a west wall drop-off located at the mid-point of Seven Mile Beach. The "nests" are actually giant barrel sponges that are intermingled with branches of staghorn coral. Some of the sponges are over 4 feet (1.2 m) tall. Check their insides and rims for cleaning gobies and coral shrimp. The wall is only 5 feet (1.5 m) from the mooring pin and starts at a depth of 60 feet (18 m). Directly below the mooring, 80 feet (24 m) down, is a large cavity in the wall hosting a huge tree of black coral.

Gray angelfish are usually seen in pairs and subsist primarily on sponges.

29. SPANISH ANCHOR

DEPTH:	40 FEET
	(12 M)

A short distance north of Aquarium Reef is another popular second dive known as Spanish Anchor. An old Spanish anchor, about 8 feet (2.5 m) long, lies embedded in the reef at a 40-foot (12 m) depth. It is well camouflaged, but it can be found by spotting the three bright yellow tube sponges attached to the metal. Divers often rub a bare spot on the anchor for good luck.

Schools of snapper and Nassau grouper are common at this reef as are angelfishes, butterflyfishes and schooling sergeant majors. Also, check under ledges for sleeping nurse sharks.

30. *DOC POLSON*

DEPTH:	60 FEET
	(18 M)

The wreck of the *Doc Polson* is a popular night dive and second dive. Also known as the Anchor Barge, the *Doc Polson* is an 80-foot-long (24 m) tugboat intentionally sunk off Seven Mile Beach. The ship is completely intact, sitting upright on the sand bottom like a classic shipwreck. All the hatches were removed to make it safe for recreational diving. You can swim through the cargo holds below deck, check out the winches and industrial equipment on top of the deck, and even get behind the controls in the wheelhouse.

At night, fishes tend to congregate more on the rear deck of the wreck. You'll see blue tang and sleeping parrotfishes. There seems to be more fishes on the *Polson* during the spring and summer months.

For a change of pace, try the reef within sight of the shipwreck which always has fish and critter action.

31. TRINITY CAVES

DEPTH:	50-100+ FEET
	(15-30+ M)

Trinity Caves ranks close to Big Tunnel in the West Wall dive site popularity standings. Three deep but narrow canyons beginning at a 60-foot (18 m) depth, slope away from shore and run off the wall at a depth just over 100 feet (30 m). The two ravines to the west converge on the top of the wall. The east canyon has a swim-through archway and leads to a large, sponge-encrusted pinnacle at the edge of the drop-off. You'll see black corals, giant basket sponges and massive barrel sponges along the wall. The top of the wall has tall formations of swaying gorgonian whips.

32. BIG TUNNEL

DEPTH:	60-100+ FEET
	(18-30+ M)

Big Tunnel is a Grand Cayman favorite. The attraction is a fascinating maze of canyons and tunnels. To find the entrance to the famous "Big Tunnel", swim southwest from the mooring around a large coral pinnacle. The tunnel is 30 feet (9 m) wide with a high opening and a flat sand bottom. Several other smaller tunnels and swim-throughs make this an interesting and exciting dive.

The face of the wall has a colorful collection of tube and vase sponges along with elephant ear sponges and bushes of black coral. Horse-eye jacks swim along the wall and tarpon hang in the caves, feeding on silversides. You may even see a spotted eagle ray glide by.

33. ORANGE CANYON

DEPTH:	50-100+ FEET
	(15-30+ M)

Bright orange elephant ear sponges and huge gorgonian fans highlight the lush formations of marine growth at Orange Canyon. Situated on a steep section of the West Wall, Orange Canyon is only 50 yards (45 m) from Bonnie's Arch heading toward Northwest Point. Look closely at the orange sponges for camouflaged frogfish. Frogfish can change color (red, yellow, orange) to blend with the background, making them difficult to spot. These odd-looking fish have an extendible lure above their upper lip for attracting food, and they are known to maintain the same resting spots for weeks.

Masses of tiny silversides fill the caverns and overhangs at Orange Canyon during the mid- and late-summer months. These silvery baitfish are a favorite prey for tarpon. When you swim through a school of silversides and they part just enough to let you pass through, you'd think you were entering another dimension. After you swim through, like mercury the silversides return to their original positions.

Spotted eagle rays and large turtles are commonly spotted off the wall at this site.

34. BONNIE'S ARCH (S)

DEPTH:	30-70 FEET
	(9-21 M)
CURRENT:	CAN BE STRONG
LEVEL:	ADVANCED

Located inshore from Orange Canyon near Northwest Point, Bonnie's Arch is famous for the impressive coral archway named in remembrance of Bonnie Charles. She was a popular underwater photographer who lived in the Caymans during the 60's and 70's.

From the mooring swim away from shore down the sloping ravine. At a depth of about 60 feet (18 m), turn right and you'll see the famous coral arch. The coral bridge spans a tunnel more than 30 feet (9 m) wide. Horse-eye jacks frequent this site and at least a dozen tarpon hang out at the arch. Watch your buoyancy because the sandy bottom stirs easily.

Turtles

Sea turtles played an important role in Cayman history. During the colonial years, sailors relied on the turtle's meat as an important source of protein. Back then, turtles were plentiful throughout the Caymans. As years passed the demand for turtle meat steadily grew. Eventually, these gentle reptiles were hunted to near extinction. Turtles are now protected by law throughout the Cayman Islands. Through government conservation efforts and the **Cayman Turtle Farm** replenishment program, there appear to be more turtles in the Caymans today than there were a decade ago. Loggerhead turtles consume squids, barnacles, jellyfishes and algae; hawksbill turtles like to eat sponges and green sea turtles feed almost entirely on sea grasses and algae. Turtles are sometimes spotted swimming through patches of sea thimbles, gulping them down like gumdrops. Unfortunately, turtles have also been known to choke on floating plastic bags that they mistake for jellyfishes.

Turtles can be seen anywhere in the Caymans, but are especially plentiful at the following sites: **Tarpon Alley**, **Orange Canyon** and **Kent's Caves** in Grand Cayman; **Strawberry Wall** in Cayman Brac; and **Bloody Bay Wall**, **Lucas Ledges** and **Splitzville** in Little Cayman.

Shore Diving

The shore diving options in Grand Cayman are a special draw for experienced divers who know the reefs and prefer to set their own schedules. Dozens of sites, including shipwrecks and wall dives, are easily reached from shore. From a purely economic standpoint, diving can be maximized at a minimum cost by opting for shore dives. Several shore diving facilities are located on the west end close to George Town, and a new facility is located near the Turtle Farm. Parrot's Landing Watersport Park, Eden Rock Dive Center, Sunset Divers, Bob Soto's, Divetech and others rent tanks and weights to certified divers, and facilitate easy access to the nearby shallow and medium depth reefs. Following are popular sites on the west end:

35. TURTLE FARM REEF (S)

DEPTH:	20-60 FEET
	(6-18 M)
CURRENT:	CAN BE STRONG

Turtle Farm Reef is one of Grand Cayman's best kept secrets. This shore entry site is located just north of the Cayman Turtle Farm. The original entry was from the ironshore; the new entry is at a recently completed concrete pier north of the Turtle Farm.

The shallow sand flats close to shore host baby peacock flounders, hundreds of tiny lettuce sea slugs, scorpionfish, sailfin blennys, scattered brain coral heads and dozens of golden sea fans. Look for the resident octopus by the entry ladder. But the main attraction is the mini-wall that runs parallel to shore. It's about a 5-minute swim from the entry point. Talk about a densely packed shallow reef dive!

The wall drops to 60 feet (18 m) and has ledges with caves, black coral bushes only 40 feet (12 m) deep, and a plethora of sponges—orange elephant ears, green fingers, black balls and pink vase. Farther out toward the main wall you'll find a stretch of sand loaded with garden eels. The instant they detect your presence they'll disappear in unison. The currents here often bring in pelagic surprises such as wahoo, Spanish mackerel and dorado.

Turtles are seen increasingly in the Caymans, thanks to conservation and restocking efforts. Enjoy the turtle's curiosity, but remember it is illegal to harrass them.

36. SUNSET REEF (S)

DEPTH: 25-55 FEET
           (8-17 M)

Sunset Reef is located 200 yards (183 m) straight off the pier at the Sunset House Hotel. It is a characteristic Cayman patch reef with scattered sponges, soft gorgonians, hard corals, and loads of small crabs and other macro life. Sunset Reef is perfect for shore night diving and is also a good site for making a warm-up or afternoon dive.

Sunset Reef also has a shipwreck to visit. The L.C.M. *David Nicholson* is a 70-foot-long (21 m) World War II landing craft intentionally sunk in 60 feet (18 m) of water. Nassau grouper, moray eels and plenty of reef tropicals make this wreck their home.

37. WALDO'S REEF (S)

DEPTH: 30-50 FEET
           (9-15 M)

Waldo's Reef, located 80 yards (73 m) straight off the dock at Coconut Harbour Hotel, is named after a famous and very tame 6-foot-long (2 m) green moray eel that once lived there. (Waldo has made the front cover of dive magazines more than once.) Now there's a new 6-foot (2 m) resident green moray as well as tame barracuda and groupers. Two friendly black groupers on the reef are named Bugsie and Blackie. The shallow reef is a typical spur-and-groove formation with ridges of coral spaced by sand channels. Gray snapper, French angelfish and loads of juveniles inhabit the reef. This site as an excellent second dive and a great night dive. After dark, look for octopus, lobster and reef squid.

37. DEVIL'S GROTTO (S)

DEPTH: 10-45 FEET
           (3-14 M)

Devil's Grotto is a fascinating tunnel dive located close to George Town, just south of Eden Rock and 150 feet (45 m) off the Parrot's Landing dock. The series of long intricate tunnels are wide enough to allow easy and safe passage. Openings in the ceiling provide sunlight to most parts of the tunnel. The silvery tarpon and swarms of shiny silversides make this a worthwhile dive. The best months for silversides in the caverns are August and September. Bring a good dive light to inspect the tunnel walls.

ADDITIONAL SHORE SITES

Other Grand Cayman shore sites include **Spanish Bay Reef [39]** at the northwest end of the island where there is access to the North Wall. Continuing east you can dive at a spot in **North Side [40]** just east of Chisolm's Grocery Store across from Pilgrim Holiness Church. If you go further east, a mile past where the roads intersect in Old Man Bay, you'll see the **Babylon Mooring [41]** about a quarter mile (.4 km) offshore.

On the south side of the islands a good spot is **Pedro's Castle [42]**.

On the west side there is access to the West Wall at **Polly's Perch [43]**, a spot 150 yards (136 m) off the Parrot's Landing dock. **Parrot's Reef [44]** is also located nearby. **Eden Rock [45]** is just south of George Town. Slightly north of George Town are the wreck of the *Cali* **[46]** and **Soto's Reef [47]**.

Caution. All Cayman shore entry wall dives are **advanced dives** and should not be attempted without proper training and guidance.

CHAPTER VII CAYMAN BRAC SITES

Dramatic walls lie on both the north and south sides of Cayman Brac. The south wall begins at 60 feet (18 m) and drops sharply to 1000-foot plus (303+ m) depths. On the north side the wall starts about 5 to 10 feet (1.5-3 m) shallower. The north wall may be a bit more lush and features numerous sand chutes that gradually cascade over the rim. The south wall definitely has more crevices and caves, and the formations inside the wall are characteristically spur and groove. Elkhorn coral stands, which are absent on the north side, are common inside the south wall at depths of 20 to 40 feet (6-12 m). Surge and swells are almost non-existent on the north side, but can be moderate on the south side since it faces thousands of miles of open sea. Also, currents are common at the sites on the far west end.

Most of the frequented sites are off the west part of Cayman Brac, close to the resorts. The reefs at the east end are, for the most part, virgin and unexplored.

North

48. AIRPORT WALL

DEPTH:	65-100 FEET
	(20-30 M)
CURRENTS:	CAN BE STRONG

Located just off Cayman Brac's westernmost tip, Airport Wall is a thrilling wall dive that starts at 65 feet (20 m), slopes gradually to 100 feet (30 m) and then plunges into an infinite blue. The top of the wall is cut with several large sandy crevices and is adorned with bunches of blue and yellow tube sponges, basket sponges and lots of large, soft gorgonian plumes and sea whips.

Friendly French angelfish roam the reef top as do schools of French grunt, horse-eye jacks and ocean triggerfish. Black, marble and Nassau grouper species can be found drifting through the reef.

Whale sharks, the largest cold-blooded animals on earth, are seen passing by this site every so often.

49. WEST CHUTE

50. MIDDLE CHUTE

51. EAST CHUTE

DEPTH:	55-100+ FEET
	(17-30+ M)
CURRENT:	MODERATE TO
	STRONG

West Chute, Middle Chute and East Chute are three separate, but similar dive sites. The "chutes" are sandy runs that spill over the drop-off east of Airport Wall. Sand flats and wide sandy clefts start at 50 to 60 feet (15-18 m) and angle down toward the wall ahead of the chutes. Enormous barrel sponges, iridescent yellow tube sponges, wire corals and rope sponges accentuate the scenic drop-offs. Schools of grunts and dog snapper hover around coral ledges while jacks and an

At depth, strawberry sponges look black in ambient light, yet when lit by artificial light, they take on a striking crimson color.

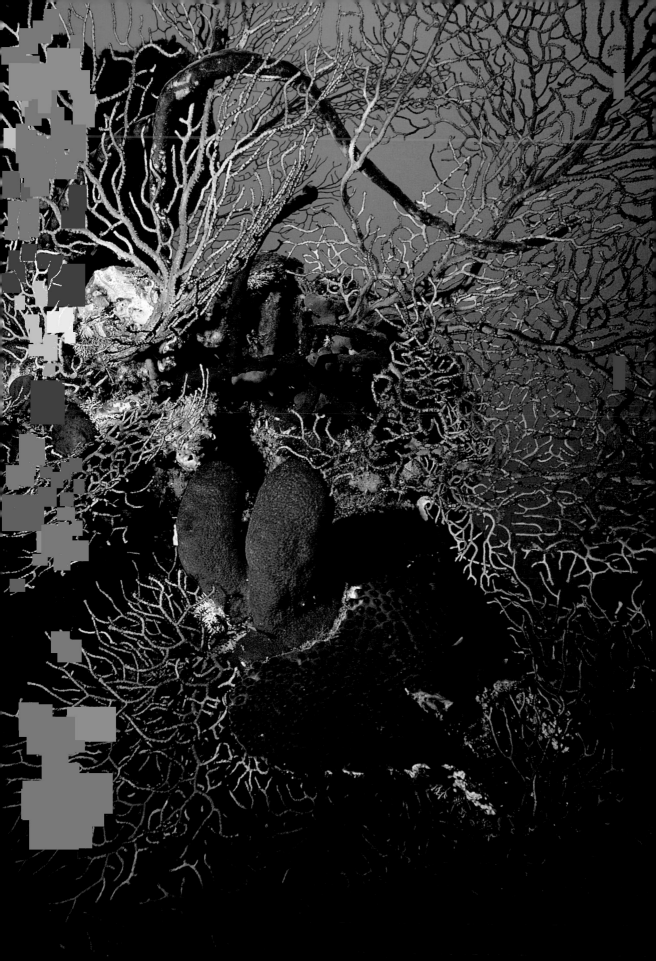

The white Russian star, reminiscent of the Cold War, remains intact under the bow hawse pipe.

Because of its enormous size, capturing major portions of the wreck requires use of an ultra wide-angle lens. A 14mm lens was used for this shot of the bridge and lower officer's quarters.

occasional eagle ray cruise along the wall.

The West Chute features a shallow mini-wall that's home for gray angelfish, butterflyfishes and rock beauties. On the East Chute, look for an old Spanish anchor embedded in the sand at 55 feet (17 m). The East Chute also has a shipwreck, the 65-foot (20 m) steel-hulled *Cayman Mariner* intentionally sunk in 1986. The intact wheelhouse makes for a fun photo prop and is home for a 150-pound (68 kg) jewfish.

52. M/V *CAPTAIN KEITH TIBBETTS* (S)

DEPTH:	20-95 FEET
	(6-29 M)

The former Russian frigate #356 was moved by tugboat from Cuba and amid much fanfare, intentionally scuttled off Cayman Brac in September 1996. The 330-foot-long (100 m)

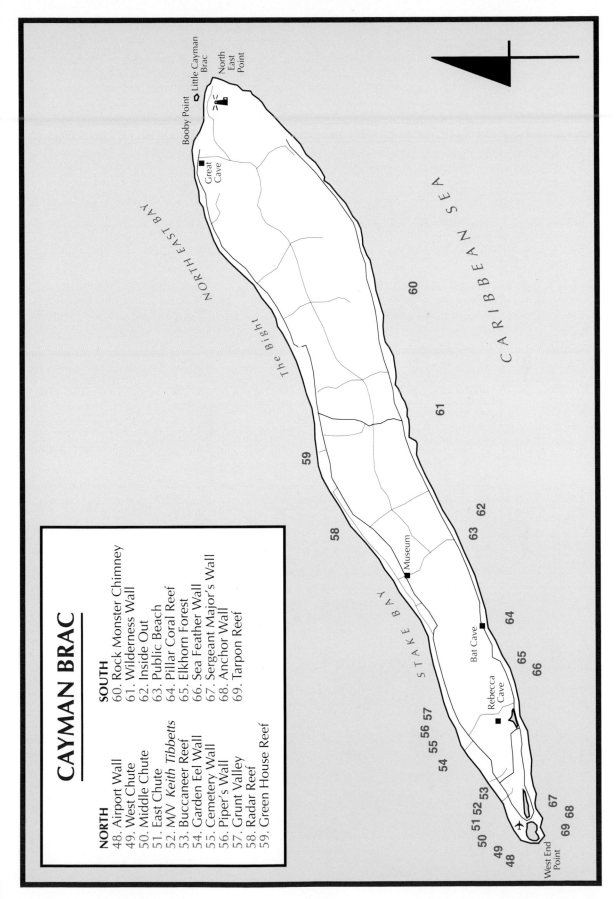

CAYMAN BRAC

NORTH
48. Airport Wall
49. West Chute
50. Middle Chute
51. East Chute
52. M/V *Keith Tibbetts*
53. Buccaneer Reef
54. Garden Eel Wall
55. Cemetery Wall
56. Piper's Wall
57. Grunt Valley
58. Radar Reef
59. Green House Reef

SOUTH
60. Rock Monster Chimney
61. Wilderness Wall
62. Inside Out
63. Public Beach
64. Pillar Coral Reef
65. Elkhorn Forest
66. Sea Feather Wall
67. Sergeant Major's Wall
68. Anchor Wall
69. Tarpon Reef

Little Cayman Brac

Booby Point

North East Point

NORTH EAST BAY

Great Cave

The Bight

CARIBBEAN SEA

60

61

59

62

63

58

Museum

64

Bat Cave

65

66

Rebecca Cave

STAKE BAY

56 57

55

54

50 51 52 53

49

48

West End Point

67

67

69 68

warship rests in a sand pocket just inside the Brac's north wall about 300 yards (273 m) straight offshore from the old Buccaneer Inn Resort. The Brigadier Type II Class Frigate was built in 1984 in Nadhodka, Russia and was renamed in honor of a popular Cayman Brac statesman. Prior to its sinking, the ship was cleaned and prepped for diver safety.

The wreck sits upright facing away from shore with the bow angled down and the hull listing slightly to port. The bow is in 95 feet (29 m) of water; amidships is at 78 feet (24 m) and the stern lies at a depth of 55 feet (17 m). Upper portions of the wreck, namely the radar tower, is in less than 20 feet (6 m) of water which allows snorkel enthusiasts to also enjoy the Cold War relic. Three permanent mooring balls are shackled to the wreck.

The starboard propeller, shaft and rudder are exposed in the sand pocket; the mid and port props are buried. Two huge turret-mounted guns on the stern and bow decks make impressive photo props. Divers can tour the upper deck and can enter the officer's quarters and the pilot house which is only 35 feet (11 m) below the surface. Most of the hardware inside the ship was removed prior to sinking, but the binnacle and helm pieces are intact. Control and navigational cabinets are open exposing the many cables once integral to the ship's operation. At amidships, lifeboat davits minus the boats, still have ropes and pulleys dangling in the current. A large Russian star is visible just below the bow hawse pipe. To avoid mishaps, crisscrossed metal bars were welded across critical openings in the main deck limiting access to the lower decks. Nearby reef residents seen on the wreck include hogfish, French angelfish and a school of silvery permit. Snorkelers will see juvenile wrasses and sergeant majors fluttering around the radar tower.

Damselfish and juvenile wrasse find refuge in the radar tower which is less than 20 feet (6 m) from the surface and accessible to snorkelers.

Divers add scale to the guns on the stern deck. On the bow are a second pair guns. Both turrets are welded to keep them from swinging.

The ship lists to port with the stern settled into the powdery sand. Of the ship's three propellers only the starboard one is exposed.

Divers should bring a wide-angle lens and dive light on this dive.

53. BUCCANEER REEF

DEPTH:	25-50 FEET
	(8-15 M)
ACCESS:	SHORE OR BOAT

Buccaneer Reef is a shore dive with an ironshore entry adjacent to the old Buccaneer Inn Hotel near the island's northwest point. The shallow reef is a basic patch reef formation. Schools of spotted eagle rays make this site their home. At night, spiny lobsters come out from under ledges, green moray eels swim through the reef, and basket stars extend their arms for feeding. Look closely for scorpionfish hiding on the bottom. Soft coral branches are meals for tiny lettuce sea slugs and the sandy areas host the unusual flying gurnards. Flying gurnards are odd-looking, gray fish with white spots, and are often found resting on the bottom. They have surprisingly large, dotted, electric-blue pectoral fins that look more like wings.

Parrotfishes, like this adult stoplight parrotfish, make crunching noises as they gnaw on corals to eat the algae inside the polyps.

54. GARDEN EEL WALL

DEPTH:	60-100 FEET
	(18-30 M)

The rim of Garden Eel Wall is adorned with plumes of soft corals and an impressive array of colorful tube and vase sponges. The most interesting marine life here are the garden eels and the southern stingrays found in the open sand flats inside the drop-off. The garden eels live in colonies and burrow in the sand with only their heads and part of their bodies visible. From a distance they look like blades of grass swaying in the currents. They are extremely shy and quickly withdraw when approached.

Southern stingrays are more approachable and will either be resting on a sandy spot or be seen cruising the sand flats. The southern rays are often accompanied by bar jacks, small shiny blue fish that reach lengths of 18 inches (46 cm).

55. CEMETERY WALL

DEPTH:	45-100+ FEET
	(14-30+ M)

Cemetery Wall, one of the shallowest and most spectacular of Cayman Brac walls, begins in 45 feet (14 m) of water just off a cemetery on the north shore. A pair of sand chutes sloping to a depth of over 100 feet (30 m) are flanked by a massive coral ridge cloaked with star corals, mounds of brain corals, swaying sea whips and loads of brown and yellow tube sponges. Huge basket sponges and bright-red finger sponges also accent the face of this breathtaking drop-off.

Nassau grouper and an occasional yellowfin grouper move through the reef and upper wall, while tiger grouper (with their "tiger bars") are often spotted motionless near ledges or shallow coral heads, taking advantage of the services of cleaning shrimp.

56. PIPER'S WALL

DEPTH:	50-100+ FEET
	(15-30+ M)

Piper's Wall is an anchor dive just east of Cemetery Wall. The top of this section of wall varies considerably in depth from 50 to 90 feet (15-27 m). A large sandy flat area in front of the drop-off leads to a huge tunnel that penetrates the face of the wall. Along the upper face you'll see a number of large

strawberry sponges. At depth, strawberry sponges appear brown or black, but when you turn on your light (or photograph with a strobe), the rich strawberry-red colors make a striking contrast to the blue water column or the reef background. Green and hawksbill turtles as well as blacktip sharks are seen at Piper's Wall on a frequent basis.

57. GRUNT VALLEY (S)

DEPTH:	20-40 FEET
	(6-12 M)

Grunt Valley, located close to shore, just east of Cemetery Wall, is an excellent site for snorkeling as well as diving. Named for the resident schools of Caesar grunts, this shallow, sloping reef features large brain and star coral heads that run perpendicular to shore. The Caesar grunts school in small groups near coral

Balloonfish have the ability to inflate their bodies and stiffen their spines to discourage predators.

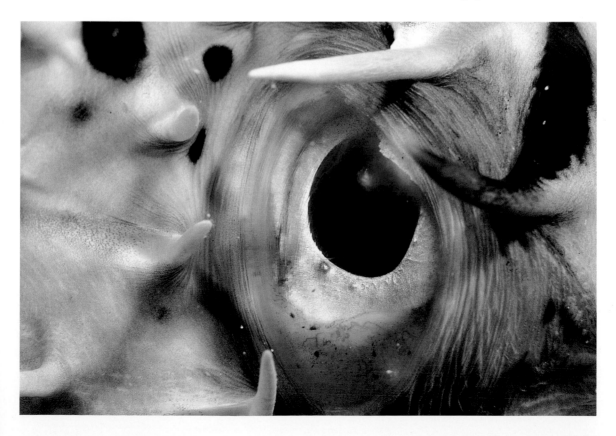

Coneys have numerous color phases that include golden, red, and this white and brown bi-color.

heads and are shy toward divers. They are easily identified by their pale blue bodies with yellow longitudinal stripes.

Grunt Valley also plays host to an array of invertebrates, in particular, file shells, banded coral shrimp and the lettuce sea slugs commonly seen on Brac reefs. These ruffled-bodied, 3-inch-long (8 cm) sea slugs get their bright blue coloration from the algae they eat. Also, closely scan the reef for camouflaged scorpionfish, and look carefully inside sponges and around their rims for neon and cleaning gobies.

Thousands of flagella propel water and nutrients through the walls of the yellow tube sponge. The tiny planktonic and organic matter are filtered and the water passes out the large opening at the end of the tubes. Sponges are great places to look for small animals which take refuge there.

58. RADAR REEF (S)

DEPTH:	25-50 FEET
	(8-15 M)
ACCESS:	SHORE OR BOAT

Radar Reef, on the north shore near the Brac Museum, can be accessed from shore or by boat. Shore entry is at the concrete boat ramp, and navigation at night to and from the reef is made easy by a long stretch of submerged phone cable. Radar Reef is a classic spur-and-groove formation with the long fingers of coral bulging from the bottom separated by sand passageways. Sea fans and gorgonian corals are plentiful and a large tunnel under the reef exits near the middle of the main formation. At night, expect to see an octopus or two, reef squid near the surface, camouflaged scorpionfish, rough file clams, red night shrimp

Diamond blennies, like this one resting on algae, use their long ventral fins and tail to support themselves like a tripod.

The shallow dive sites on Cayman Brac's south side are riddled with caves and ledges that are often inhabited by nurse sharks.

and numerous sleeping parrotfishes. Grunts, Bermuda chub and gray snapper are common in small schools near ledges and large coral heads.

There's as good or better chance of seeing the unusual flying gurnards in the sand areas of Radar Reef as there is at Buccaneer.

Approach feather duster worms slowly because they vanish into their tubes when disturbed.

59. GREEN HOUSE REEF (S)

DEPTH:	25-60 FEET
	(8-18 M)

As you might guess, Green House Reef is named for the green house directly onshore from the site. Green House Reef is one of the easternmost sites on the north shore and is situated between Jan's Reef and Plymouth Rock (named for an old rusted Plymouth on shore). The bottom has a gradual slope in the 25- to 60-foot (8-18 m) range making it an excellent choice for snorkeling or a second dive of the day.

Check out the sand areas for queen conch and small burrowing fishes. Several crevices that cut through the coral also host an abundance of small critters. Expect to see

Most of Cayman Brac's population live on the island's north side; the south side has miles of nearly deserted beaches.

spider crabs, spiny lobsters, banded coral shrimp and arrow crabs. Consider this site a macro bonanza. Photographers should be equipped with macro lenses or extension tubes.

Green House Reef also hosts eels—big green moray eels as well as the sharptail snake eels. The snake eels have thin, gray bodies with small yellow spots on their heads. Under ledges you can occasionally spot sleeping nurse sharks.

SOUTH

60. ROCK MONSTER CHIMNEY

DEPTH:	45-100 FEET
	(14-30 M)

Rock Monster Chimney is the shallowest drop-

off on the south side of Cayman Brac. The inside patch reefs and sand areas are 50 feet (15 m) deep, but toward the wall, the bottom contour gradually rises to a minimum depth of 45 feet (14 m) near the edge of the drop-off. Loads of feathery soft corals decorate the upper face of the sloping wall. Blue and brown chromis, and schools of purple creole wrasse hover over the corals. Fast-moving schools of horse-eye jacks swirl around the reef in unison. Spotted eagle rays work the sandy areas uncovering delectable mollusks.

This site has several large canyons with sloping tunnels and chimneys that penetrate the reef at about 50 feet (15 m) and exit the wall at depths of 80 to 110 feet (24-33 m).

Confident of their armor and powerful claws, blue crabs are pugnacious and often become aggressive when approached.

61. WILDERNESS WALL

DEPTH: 60-100+ FEET
(18-30+ M)

Wilderness Wall is located in the Brac's eastern "wilderness." Touted as one of Cayman Brac's most dramatic walls, this site features an enormous rounded coral pinnacle set off from a recess in the wall. The edge of the wall is 60 feet (18 m) deep and the top of the pinnacle is 80 feet (24 m) below the surface about 50 feet (15 m) across. Schools of silvery horse-eye jacks are often seen between the wall and the giant outcropping. The pinnacle and adjacent wall have thick covers of corals and sponges. Several crevices and swim-throughs penetrate the face of the wall. Schools of blue tang cruise along the reef top while stoplight parrotfish patrol leisurely between the coral heads.

62. INSIDE OUT

DEPTH: 60-100+ FEET
(18-30+ M)

Inside Out features a sheer drop-off with an upward projection at the lip of the wall that creates a shallower mini-wall on the inside.

The bulge in the outer reef has two caves. The first cave opening is at 80 feet (24 m) and runs horizontal to the outer drop-off; the second, deeper tunnel starts at 90 feet (27 m) and slopes off the wall to over 110 feet (33 m). Count on seeing large schools of creole wrasse and blue chromis flitting above the wall. Creole wrasse are fish 4 to 6 inches (10-15 cm) long and have purple bodies with dark foreheads. Their schools seem to be in constant motion.

Keep checking off the wall for eagle rays and

A royal poinciana tree adds color and shade to this modest homestead in Cayman Brac.

other pelagics. Several pretty stands of golden elkhorn coral are located in the shallower section of reef.

63. PUBLIC BEACH (S)

DEPTH: 35-100+ FEET

(11-30+ M)

Situated directly off Cayman Brac's public beach, this buoyed site starts in a shallow sandy area less than 40 feet (12 m) deep. The bottom slopes gradually toward the wall's precipice at a depth of 60 feet (18 m). The scenery on the swim to the wall features sand chutes, swim-throughs and coral ledges with gorgonians, tube sponges and fans. Look for ruffled lettuce sea slugs on the reef and in the sandy areas. Head southwest toward the Inside Out mooring for more fish activity.

64. PILLAR CORAL REEF

DEPTH: 25-60 FEET

(8-18 M)

Three prominent pillar coral formations give this shallow reef its name. Located just off the Coral Isle Club, Pillar Coral Reef is a convoluted formation of coral spurs and sand grooves with small caves, cuts and alleyways. The 60-foot (18 m) depth makes this site suitable for a second dive.

Giant Caribbean pink-tipped anemones often host tiny cleaner and pistol shrimps as well as diamond blennies. The tips of their tentacles contain stinging cells.

Elkhorn coral is a type of hard coral
that gets its name because its yellow
branches resemble antlers. They are
very sturdy and thrive in shallow
water in or near the surf zone.

Along the south side of Cayman Brac are some of the most magnificent stands of elkhorn coral in the Caribbean. Some colonies can reach a height of 12 feet (4 m).

Check the sandy areas for yellow stingrays resting on the bottom. They are often covered with sand and well camouflaged. In the crevices or under the ledges here you can find spiny lobsters, green moray eels or resting nurse sharks. There are friendly Nassau grouper, schools of yellowtail snapper and Bermuda chub to enjoy. Bermuda chub are silver, oval-shaped fish 1 to 2 feet (31-62 cm) long. They often swim fast and school in tight formations, making rapid turns in unison.

65. ELKHORN FOREST (S)

DEPTH: 20-50 FEET

            (6-15 M)

Elkhorn corals are seen at many of Cayman Brac's south sites, but the stands seen at

Elkhorn Forest are some of Cayman's biggest and best. The golden-brown hard corals thrive on the shallow reef tops in 20 to 35 feet (6-11 m) of water. A network of sand channels cuts through the shallow reef and slope to a maximum depth of 50 feet (15 m). Numerous crevices and small caves host eels, crabs and lobsters. Look for nurse sharks under ledges and inside the larger openings of the reef. Sometimes scorpionfish are seen camouflaged against the small hard corals. The sand and rubble areas host tiny burrowing jawfish, resting stingrays and foraging eagle rays. Other reef fishes include tiger groupers, spotfin butterflys and swarms of sergeant major damsels.

66. SEA FEATHER WALL

DEPTH:	70-100+ FEET
	(21-30+ M)

This is one of the Brac's steeper south shore sites located less than five minutes from either Brac resort. The top of the wall starts at 70 feet (21 m) and is generously adorned with brown and yellow sponges intermingled with soft gorgonian corals. You'll also see several large basket sponges near the edge of the wall. At a depth of 95 feet (29 m), caves and openings in the wall slope upward to sand chutes and tunnels. Resident fishes include Nassau groupers, queen triggerfish, orange filefish and schooling blue chromis. The blue chromis often school near the surface where they feed on plankton.

Tiny lettuce sea slugs cloaked in pale blue ruffles, are commonly spotted in the crevices along the top of the wall. Look for the trails they cut as they feed on soft corals.

67. SERGEANT MAJOR'S WALL (S)

DEPTH:	20-60 FEET
	(6-18 M)

Sergeant Major's Wall was named for the swarms of chevron-striped damsels that filled the water column when the mooring was originally installed. The sergeant majors have moved on, but there's certainly no shortage of other reef fishes.

This site is located directly off a point

Crinoids, also called sea lilies or feather stars, use their long arms to trap plankton from the water column. They also have the ability to swim freely.

midway between the two resorts which means the boat ride there is less than one minute. The top of the reef is a mere 20 feet (6 m) deep and has beautifully formed sea fans, soft whips and hard elkhorns. The numerous cuts, channels and tunnels make this site interesting to explore. Schooling fishes include snappers, goatfishes, yellow wrasse, black durgons and blue chromis. Squirrelfishes hide under the ledges and large numbers of schoolmasters pack themselves beneath the elkhorn stands. Spotted eagle rays are often seen cruising along the sandy channels on their way to the inshore lagoon.

68. ANCHOR WALL

DEPTH:	75-100+ FEET
	(23-30+ M)
CURRENT:	MODERATE TO
	STRONG

Only a minute or two by boat from either Brac resort, Anchor Wall is an exciting drop-off that starts at 75 feet (23 m). As you approach the bottom, you'll see a number of deep crevices and small tunnels that run from the sand flats through the ridge of the wall. The face of the craggy wall spouts blue sea fans, loads of soft gorgonians and dazzling blue tube sponges.

The signature of this site is a 10-foot-long (3 m) old English wrought-iron anchor that is fused to the reef at a depth of 100 feet (30 m). Bring your camera and wide-angle lens. This colorful (when lit artificially) coral and sponge-encrusted anchor makes an excellent photo prop. Use a diver to add scale to your shot. Also, be sure to keep an eye out for rays and turtles cruising through this site.

69. TARPON REEF

DEPTH:	30-60 FEET
	(9-18 M)
CURRENT:	MILD TO
	MODERATE

Tarpon Reef, located near the southwest tip of the island, is a shallow spur-and-groove formation. The "spurs" are strips of coral protruding from the bottom; the "grooves" are the separations, usually sandy areas, that are between the spurs. A dozen or more silvery tarpon can usually be seen hovering over, or cruising through the sand gullies. Move slowly and you can get a close look at these magnificent fish. You'll be impressed by their large armor-plated scales and the long filaments streaming from the base of their dorsal fins. Tarpon Reef also has several spectacular stands of pillar coral, a hard coral with a wide base and rising spires of brown fuzzy polyps. Unlike most corals, pillar coral extend their polyps during the day.

ADDITIONAL SNORKEL SITES

If you've never been close to a spotted eagle ray and want a sure thing, go snorkeling near the piers at **Dive Tiara** or **Brac Reef** early in the evening. If you prefer to stay dry, you can see them pass by while standing on the dock.

Spotted eagle rays reach wing spans of up to 8 feet (2.5 m) and are easily recognized by their exceptionally long, slender tails and dark backs patterned with white circular rings. They are generally shy and difficult to approach except when they are feeding. Eagle rays feed on mollusks and worms they uncover as they patrol the sandy bottom.

Cayman Brac operators schedule a number of boat trips each week to Little Cayman's Bloody Bay and Jackson's Bay sites.

CHAPTER VIII LITTLE CAYMAN SITES

Most who have dived throughout the Caribbean agree that Little Cayman's Bloody Bay Wall is as good as it gets. At several places this breathtaking wall, lush with corals and sponges, starts at depths of less than 20 feet (6 m). The sites along the wall are visited by relatively few divers and the formations are pristine.

Most of the frequented sites are protected by the government and only boats smaller than 60 feet (18 m) long can drop anchor in the protected areas. Larger vessels are required to use any of the more than 20 moorings.

Off the north shore, currents are usually nonexistent and visibility often exceeds 150 feet (45 m). The south side of the island features a deeper, sloping wall with numerous reef sites that are dived when the wind blows from the north.

Bloody Bay Wall runs along the far northwestern shoreline. The top of this legendary drop-off is the shallowest in the Caymans and the face is a sheer cliff. Jackson's Bay, just east of Bloody Bay, has a sloping main wall and a shallow, inner reef mini-wall. The drop-offs at Jackson start at 40 feet (12 m) and fall to over 1,000 feet (300 m). A wide sandy channel runs parallel to shore just inside the Jackson's Bay Wall. The sand flats host garden eels, stingrays, eagle rays and schooling reef fishes. It's common to see eagle rays cruising along Grand Cayman's North Wall, but in Little Cayman, eagle rays feed in the sand alleys and are approachable. Swim-through chimneys are found all along the fringe of Jackson's Bay Reef and the face of the wall is thick with corals and sponges.

NORTH

Bloody Bay

70. JOY'S JOY (S)

DEPTH:	20-100+ FEET
	(6-30+ M)

Joy's Joy is a wall and shallow reef dive located east of Salt Rocks on the far west end of Bloody Bay. Take your time and swim slowly at this site or you will miss the little surprises. Small corkscrew anemones, arrow crabs and coral shrimp hide out in the crevices and holes that riddle the shallows and the wall. Parallel troughs of sand spill over the wall between fingers of outcropping coral. Along the upper face of the wall you'll see an adornment of crayola-colored tube and vase sponges as well as plumes of soft corals. Numerous small burrowing fishes and a variety of invertebrates such as spiny lobsters, spider crabs and octopuses hide in the shallows close to shore.

Big tube sponges, like these at Jackson's Bight, abound on the sheer walls of Little Cayman. Fairy basslets are often seen swimming "upside down" along the reef, and under ledges and cave ceilings.

Little Cayman has a combination post office and air terminal with an open-air passenger lounge at its unpaved Edward Bodden Airfield.

71. COCONUT WALK (S)

DEPTH:	30-100+ FEET
	(9-30+ M)

This section of Bloody Bay, like Joy's Joy, has a series of crevices and coral outcroppings at the approach to the wall. Enormous bowl and barrel sponges accent the wall as do yellow tube sponges, lavender vase sponges and purple soft corals. Swim west of the mooring to see an impressive stand of hard, pillar coral. Pillar coral is one of the few corals that extend their polyps during the day and night. Look for giant anemones, most notably the green-tipped variety, in the flats and on the wall. Peterson cleaner shrimp, diamond blennys and striped arrow crabs are often found within the host anemones. Sailfin blennys, juvenile reef fishes and a host of other small critters inhabit the shallows.

A sailfin blenny is a 2-inch (5 cm) long black fish with exceptionally long dorsal fins. They live in sand burrows and are usually found with only their heads sticking out. If you wait long enough, you'll see them dart out of their holes and for a split second, flick their dorsal "sails" up and down. Just as fast, they then back into their burrows, tail first.

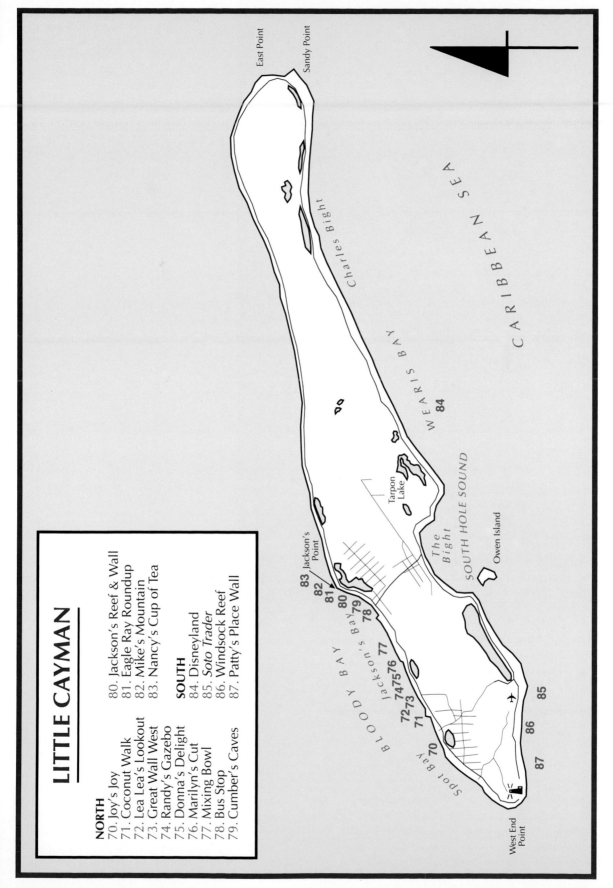

LITTLE CAYMAN

NORTH
70. Joy's Joy
71. Coconut Walk
72. Lea Lea's Lookout
73. Great Wall West
74. Randy's Gazebo
75. Donna's Delight
76. Marilyn's Cut
77. Mixing Bowl
78. Bus Stop
79. Cumber's Caves

80. Jackson's Reef & Wall
81. Eagle Ray Roundup
82. Mike's Mountain
83. Nancy's Cup of Tea

SOUTH
84. Disneyland
85. *Soto Trader*
86. Windsock Reef
87. Patty's Place Wall

East Point

Sandy Point

Charles Bight

CARIBBEAN SEA

WEARIS BAY

84

Tarpon Lake

SOUTH HOLE SOUND

The Bight

Owen Island

Jackson's Point

83

82
81
80
79
78
77
76
75
74
73
72
71
70

BLOODY BAY

Jackson's Bay

Spot Bay

85
86
87

West End Point

The impressive diversity of colorful corals and sponges at Bloody Bay make it one of the Caribbean's best wall dives.

72. LEA LEA'S LOOKOUT (S)

DEPTH: 30-100+ FEET

(9-30+ M)

Heading east along Bloody Bay Wall, the inside sand flats gradually deepen. At Lea Lea's Lookout, the boat mooring is 45 feet (14 m) deep. Instead of swimming due north to the wall, head west until you reach a trough that widens and drops to a deep canyon ending at the wall. This section of Bloody Bay Wall has enormous barrel sponges, large red cup sponges and blue- and pink-tipped anemones. One particular barrel sponge on the wall at 65 feet (20 m) has so many gobies crowded around its rim that if you stretch your hand out, several gobies will hop off on your arm to get more room. Numerous stands of black coral along with orange elephant ear sponges also accent the face of the wall at the 60- to 100-foot (18-30 m) range. Expect to see schools of

These colorful lavender, brown and golden filter feeding sponges on the Great Wall compete for space with neighboring corals.

horse-eye jacks rushing through the reef. Spotted moray eels often hide out at the edge of the wall near the mooring. The sandy shallows host sailfin blennys, yellowhead jawfish and sand tilefish.

Sand tilefish are pale yellow or blue fish with very long anal and dorsal fins that undulate continuously as they hover close to their burrows. They tend to be nervous, so if you get too close, they dart head first into their holes.

73. GREAT WALL WEST (S)

DEPTH:	30-100+ FEET
	(9-30+ M)

Bloody Bay's Great Wall West may be the most sensational sheer wall dive in the Caymans if not the entire Caribbean. The top of the wall is 30 feet (9 m) below the surface and the face is so vertically smooth, it looks

Whitestar cardinalfish are nocturnal and are often found in and around sponges.

Fire sponges are a type of encrusting sponge that can be irritating to the skin if touched.

like it was sheared by a giant guillotine. The size and profusion of sponges and sea fans are a delight. At depths of more than 80 feet (24 m), the platinum yellow tube sponges appear to glow in the deep blue backdrop. Red finger sponges are plentiful along the wall as are pink and azure cup sponges, cream-colored vase sponges, and enormous bushes of black coral found 80 to 90 feet (24-27 m) deep. Don't be surprised to see a spotted eagle ray, blacktip shark or other pelagic fish cruising along the wall.

A colony of star corals feeds at night on plankton using their extended tentacles to paralyze their microscopic prey. During the day they retract their tentacles.

74. RANDY'S GAZEBO (S)

DEPTH:	30-100+ FEET
	(9-30+ M)

The mooring at Randy's Gazebo (also known as the Chimneys) is located at the edge of a wide recess in the wall just east of Bloody Bay Point. Inside this recessed section, two vertical caves or "chimneys" penetrate the face of the wall. Follow the mooring line to the bottom and you'll see the exit to the first chimney whose entrance is just a short distance straight down the wall. To find the main chimney, swim west of the mooring until you see a large pinnacle near the top of the wall. Just before

Cayman reefs host numerous species of brittle stars which are often found inside sponges and around soft corals.

reaching the pinnacle, look for an opening at around 40 feet (12 m). Follow the sloping tunnel down to the exit on the wall at 75 feet (23 m). Now head east along the wall about 100 feet (30 m) or so maintaining a 75-foot (23 m) depth and you'll find a dramatic coral formation known as "the gazebo." An archway cuts through the top of the formation and a large mound of flower coral can be seen just east of the gazebo. The gazebo provides a good wide-angle photo opportunity to shoot a diver swimming through the archway.

When ascending near the rim of the wall, keep an eye out for green-tipped anemones hosting pistol shrimp, arrow crabs and other macro critters. The shallow reef inshore from the wall is a virtual garden of soft corals where gray angelfish and rock beauties meander, while schools of yellow goatfish probe the sand bottom with their barbels to uncover food.

75. DONNA'S DELIGHT (S)

DEPTH:	30-100+ FEET
	(9-30+ M)

The vertical drop at Donna's Delight, which is also called Black Coral Forest, starts at 30 feet (9 m) and plummets to well past 100 feet (30 m). Actually, the wall in front of the mooring is sloping; east and west of the mooring, the wall gets steeper.

Red cup sponges are abundant and the brilliant yellow tube sponges visually jump out from the rest of the lush growth on the wall. Several large stands of black coral sprout from the wall 60 to 100 feet (18-30 m) down. Nassau grouper swim along the wall at medium and shallow depths, and dense schools of blue chromis hover above the top of

Large schools of purple creole wrasse soar in constant motion across Little Cayman's reeftops plucking plankton from the currents.

the wall. You'll also see spotted moray eels hiding out in crevices at the edge of the wall near the mooring. The shallow, sandy flats host camouflaged peacock flounders, sailfin blennys and the odd-looking flying gurnards. Look for flamingo tongue snails with their orange-spotted mantles on the branches of soft coral. They leave distinct trails as they feed along the coral.

76. MARILYN'S CUT (S)

DEPTH:	20-100+ FEET
	(6-30+ M)

Marilyn's Cut, also called Hole in the Wall, is located just east of Donna's Delight. From the boat mooring which is only 15 feet (5 m) deep, head down the gradually sloping bottom to the rim of the wall. Swimming west of the mooring along the wall, you'll approach a rounded mass of protruding coral. Deep fissures widening to canyons separate the coral pinnacle from the wall. The entrance to the "hole in the wall" is in a canyon just east of the pinnacle. The swim-through chimney exits at 25 feet (8 m). As you fin along the wall, you'll pass black coral bushes and several huge barrel sponges. The multi-hued tube sponges here are plentiful and especially photogenic. While swimming along the wall at the 60- to 70-foot (18-21 m) level, look closely at the gorgonians and you might spot a sea horse.

Huge jewfish and the smaller more approachable Nassau grouper are common along the wall. You'll find two of the regulars, nicknamed Ben and Freddy, especially photogenic. Don't be surprised to come across a nurse shark in the shallow inner reef area you'll visit at the end of the dive.

Jackson's Bay

77. MIXING BOWL (S)

DEPTH:	15-100+ FEET
	(5-30+ M)

Mixing Bowl, also known as Three Fathom Wall, is where Bloody Bay meets Jackson's Bay. The face of the wall transitions from Bloody Bay's sheer vertical plane to the more gradual sloping drop-off characteristic of Jackson. Mixing Bowl, unlike any other Little Cayman site, has the best of both bays—spectacular, take-your-breath-away walls with ledges, cuts, crevices, sand alleys, and the shallower inshore mini-wall and sand flats typical of Jackson's Bay.

The top of the main wall, fringed with feathery sea whips and soft coral plumes, is a mere 18 feet (5.5 m) or 3 fathoms below the surface. It's one of the easiest walls to snorkel

You can usually find schools of blue striped grunts at Mixing Bowl. Sometimes you can hear grunting noises when they grind their teeth.

CAYMAN LIVEABOARDS

In 1979 the Caribbean's first modern liveaboard dive boat cast off from a George Town pier. Since then the popularity of unlimited, no-hassle diving has spiraled. On a liveaboard it takes only minutes and a few steps to get wet. And there's no back and forth with cameras and bags of dive gear. Staying on one of these floating dive resorts also provides more freedom and flexibility for setting your diving schedule.

If your idea of a vacation is dive-dive-dive and you can handle spending a week on a large yacht, then liveaboards are meant for you. Four dives a day are common and if carefully planned, five including one after dark can be made.

More important than the quantity of bottom time liveaboards allow, is the quality of dives. Liveaboards visit many of the remote sites that are outside the range of most day boats.

Two liveaboard dive boats operate in the Cayman Islands. The **Cayman Aggressor III** docks in George Town, Grand Cayman, and dives its north and east walls as well as Bloody Bay Wall in Little Cayman. The **Little Cayman Diver II** berths in Cayman Brac but spends the entire week at Little Cayman sites.

If the liveaboard concept sounds appealing but you're not quite sure about your sea legs, consider an all-day trip aboard Sunset Diver's **Manta**.

---

in the entire Caribbean. Schooling jacks, blue tang, angelfishes and hawksbill turtles are often seen at this site. Look up to see dense schools of bright blue chromis feeding near the surface. Swim east of the mooring to see large schools of French and Caesar grunts, schoolmasters and other snappers hanging under the shallow ledges.

Friendly grouper like to hang under the dive boat. The golden coney, a smaller member of the grouper family, is another likely encounter. Look for a blue-speckled, brilliant yellow fish that's about 10 inches (26 cm) long and shaped like a grouper. Scorpionfish, sand tilefish, southern rays and yellowhead jawfish reside in the shallows.

78. BUS STOP

DEPTH:	45-100+ FEET
	(14-30+ M)

Bus Stop, named for an old bus in the bushes on shore, is a near-perfect Jackson's Bay formation with a sand corridor inside the wall's fringing reef line and an inshore mini-wall that runs parallel to the main wall. A large pocket of sand, just west of the mooring, funnels off the wall. For your first deep dive, follow this path to the wall. On your second dive, swim due north from the mooring to find a coral ledge that is home to juvenile drum. In the sand at the base of the mini-wall, you'll see peacock flounders, garden eels, yellowhead jawfish and southern rays accompanied by bar jacks. For smaller critters, check out the rims of barrel sponges for gobies or inspect a pink-

Schoolmasters, a type of snapper known for their prominent canine teeth, like to congregate in shadows under ledges.

The bridled burrfish is a spiny-type puffer that has powerful jaws used to crush shelled invertebrates.

Trumpetfish ambush their prey and are often seen motionless, head down in a vertical position amongst the branches of gorgonians or sea whips.

tipped anemone for shrimp and decorator crabs. This is also a good site for tiger grouper and schooling French grunt.

79. CUMBER'S CAVES (S)

DEPTH:	12-100+ FEET
	(4-30+ M)

Cumber's Caves has four parallel swim-through tunnels that can be entered inside the wall at a depth of 50 feet (15 m). They exit the wall at 100 feet (30 m). An old anchor marks the entrance to the westernmost cave. Look for spotted eagle rays, hawksbill turtles, queen triggerfish, rainbow parrotfish and an occasional blacktip shark swimming off the wall. This is the area that the famous manta ray named Molly, frolicked at night off and on for more than four years. She loved to feed on plankton and perform playful loops with mouth agape and frontal fins unfurled. Molly was last seen in the fall of 1995.

The mini-wall at this site is well formed and rises to within 12 feet (3.6 m) of the surface. The sand channel that runs parallel between the two walls is 40 feet (12 m) deep and approximately 80 feet (24 m) wide. This sandy corridor is home to garden eels, queen conchs and yellowhead jawfish. There's probably more jawfish in this area than anywhere else along Jackson's Bay. Southern stingrays with accompanying bar jacks, and yellow goatfish feed along these sand flats.

Flamingo tongue snails are often found feeding on gorgonians. Their leopard-like spots are actually part of their mantles and not their shells.

80. JACKSON'S REEF AND WALL (S)

DEPTH:	30-100+ FEET
	(9-30+ M)

There's much more to see at Jackson's Reef and Wall than a single dive will allow. This site is also called Jackson's Bight and there always seems to be a few more fishes and critters here, perhaps because of its special location smack in the middle of Jackson's Bay. The drop-off begins at 35 feet (11 m) and the face of the wall is riddled with so many swim-throughs and tunnels it looks like a mass of Swiss cheese. Overhead you'll notice schools of blue chromis and swirling horse-eye jacks. The shallow inside reef has a mini-wall formation just east of the mooring, where butterflyfishes, angelfishes and juvenile tropicals can be seen.

81. EAGLE RAY ROUNDUP (S)

DEPTH:	15-100+ FEET
	(5-30+ M)

Southern stingrays and, as the name implies, spotted eagle rays cruise through the shallow sand alleys at Eagle Ray Roundup. The sand flats begin to slope down near the lip of the wall forming a series of spillways that cut through the coral rim. Numerous fissures, tunnels and craggy growths of hard corals accentuate this section of Jackson's Reef.

Head west from the mooring to find two old ship anchors behind the wall at a depth of 40 feet (12 m). Colonies of sinuous garden eels make their burrows in the flats south of the permanent mooring.

82. MIKE'S MOUNTAIN (S)

DEPTH:	18-100+ FEET
	(5-30+ M)

Mike's Mountain is within swimming distance from Nancy's Cup of Tea. The mooring is 18 feet deep (5.5 m) and the boat normally floats over a large pocket of sand just inside the fringing reef. In the side of the sand pocket, close to the wall, is the entrance to a tunnel that penetrates the reef and exits the wall at 85 feet (26 m). A large tree of black coral is attached to the cavern at the exit.

Follow the wall east (toward Nancy's) and you'll approach a large protruding coral overhang. Just above this overhang is a favorite cleaning station for groupers. You may see juvenile hogfish servicing a line-up of Nassau, tiger and black groupers. Fairy basslets and juvenile bluehead wrasses flit around the coral heads, while black durgons roam the reef and brown chromis feed on plankton near the surface.

Swim south along the mini-wall to find yellow stingrays resting on the bottom and tiny, black sailfin blennys poking out of their sand burrows. Other burrowers, male yellowhead jawfish, can be found with mouths stuffed full of eggs in the rubble areas near the base of the mini-wall. A large community of bashful garden eels reside west of the mooring between the mini-wall and drop-off.

83. NANCY'S CUP OF TEA (S)

DEPTH:	35-100+ FEET
	(11-30+ M)
CURRENT:	CAN BE STRONG

Located just west of Jackson's Point, this site is named after underwater photographer and former Little Cayman resident, Nancy Sefton. This unusual site is also called Magic Roundabout and has two parallel canyons that lead to a huge circular outcropping off the main wall. This "magic roundabout" or "cup of tea" pinnacle, profuse with tube sponges, large elephant ear sponges and soft gorgonian corals, tops off at a depth of 50 feet (15 m). Swim the perimeter of the pinnacle to find several bushes of black coral at the 60- to 80-foot (18-24 m) range. Large animals such as hawksbill turtles and spotted eagle rays frequent this stretch of Jackson's Bay. Head to the shallows to find spotted goatfish, hogfish, sand tilefish and other small burrowing fish. An old cannon can be inspected east of the mooring at a 30-foot (9 m) depth.

Caution. From this site and further east, currents can be strong.

At Nancy's Cup of Tea, a diver inspects yellow sponges for tube-dwelling fish and critters.

SOUTH

When the wind picks up from the northwest which occurs more often in the winter, operators head for Little Cayman's south side. The south walls start deeper, and are not as steep and shear as the north walls.

84. DISNEYLAND

DEPTH:	65-100+ FEET
	(20-30+ M)

Disneyland may be the best deep dive site on Little Cayman's south side. Two tunnels, one on each side of the mooring, penetrate the wall and exit at 110 feet (33 m). Blacktip sharks, spotted eagle rays and hawksbill turtles are possible pelagic encounters at this site.

The shallow sand areas above the drop-off host yellowhead jawfish and sand tilefish. The chain moray eel, a rarity in the Caymans, is sometimes spotted poking out of a hole near a shallow coral head. Look for a small dark eel about the size of a goldentail eel, except it has a thicker body with bright yellow, chain-like patterns.

85. *SOTO TRADER*

DEPTH:	40-50 FEET
	(12-15 M)

The *Soto Trader* was an island freighter that caught fire and sunk in a 50-foot-deep (15 m) sand pocket just outside the South Sound Main Channel. The 140-foot-long (42 m) wreck lies upright and is well intact. There's plenty of ambient light for exploring the engine room, crew quarters and cargo hold, but the visibility is usually less than 60 feet (18 m). Several large jewfish make this wreck their home, and during August and September, clouds of silversides fill the wreck. The grouper and jewfish love it.

The best dives on the *Soto* are at night. You'll see sleeping parrotfishes, free-swimming morays and roaming octopuses. Shipwreck and fish photo opportunities are exceptional. The nearby reef has a resident 12-inch (31 cm) spotted drum, and spotted eagle rays are often seen gliding by.

86. WINDSOCK REEF (S)

DEPTH:	30-50 FEET
	(9-15 M)

Windsock Reef, located due south of Little Cayman's grass airstrip, is a spur-and-groove formation featuring mounds of mountainous star corals that overlap with brain coral heads creating a melted wax appearance. This shallow site also has numerous ledges and small arches where eels, lobsters and a host of juvenile fishes find refuge. Look for purple and white lettuce sea slugs inching their way along the reef in and out of crevices as they feed on algae. A large school of shiny tarpon often hang in the area between the arches and the shore.

87. PATTY'S PLACE WALL (S)

DEPTH:	60-100+ FEET
	(18-30+ M)

The approach to Patty's Place Wall is a sandy plain with coral fingers that run perpendicular to the shoreline. The top of the wall is at 60 feet (18 m) and has a series of chimneys that begin near the lip and drop to exits at 100 feet (30 m). An encounter with a nurse shark or a spotted eagle ray is a distinct possibility at this site.

The shallow sandy areas inside the wall host groups of tiny jawfish that hover over their burrows in anticipation of snagging a micro meal. Other noteworthy reef inhabitants include spotted moray eels, black grouper and Nassau grouper.

CHAPTER **IX** MARINE LIFE

The variety of interesting and exciting marine life found in Cayman waters is unrivaled in the Western Hemisphere. Some of the animals are interactive, others tend to be shy and require patience for a close look or photograph. The following are just a few of the shining stars in Cayman's nearly endless constellation of marine animals.

Flying Gurnards

The odd-looking **flying gurnard** (*Dactylopterus volitans*) appears almost like a cross between a slim cowfish and a sea robin—blunt head, large eyes and wings. Flying gurnards are commonly seen at Buccaneer Reef, a Cayman Brac shore dive on the north side. Look for them in the sandy areas where they feed on crustaceans. Flying gurnards have blue and white spots, and a magnificent body pattern. Several sites along Little Cayman's Jackson's Bay also host these unusual fish.

Garden Eels

Garden eels (*Heteroconger halis*) are small, slender eels 8 to 15 inches (21-39 cm) long that are found in sandy areas close to reefs. Garden eels live in colonies. From a distance they appear like swaying blades of gray grass. These fascinating creatures are members of the Congridae family. Their bodies are dark brown to gray, and they have distinctive lower jaws and proportionally large eyes. Easily frightened by bubbles or movement, garden eels will quickly retract tail first into their burrows for safety. The sand flats near the *Oro Verde* host garden eels as does Garden Eel Wall in Cayman Brac. Numerous dives along Little Cayman's Jackson's Wall also host large colonies of garden eels.

Groupers

Nearly every popular Cayman dive site has a resident grouper or two. The most common variety is the **Nassau grouper** (*Epinephelus striatus*). Groupers are solid, stocky fish with large mouths and lips. The Nassau grouper is easily identified by the brownish body with cream colored bands along its side and head. They also have a black spot at the base of their tail and freckles around their eyes and lips. Nassau groupers are tame fish that like to be fed. But make no mistake about their power. Teasing a grouper with food can be very dangerous to your health.

Groupers have an affinity for shipwrecks. Certain dive sites like the wreck of the *Oro Verde* have resident groupers with nicknames. Other grouper sites in Grand Cayman are Sunset Reef, Parrot's Reef and Grouper Grotto. Marilyn's Cut and Jackson's Reef in Little Cayman are also good sites for seeing groupers. Other grouper varieties found in Cayman are the giant **jewfish** (*Epinephelus itajara*) that grow to lengths of 7 feet (2 m), the **black grouper** (*Mycteroperca bonaci*) seen at Waldo's Reef and Jackson's Point, and the striking **tiger grouper** (*Mycteroperca tigris*), identified by the nine brown tiger bars over a pale body. Tiger groupers are commonly seen along the north walls of all three islands. The **yellow phase coney** (*Epinephelus fulvus*), another grouper family member, can be seen regularly at Little Cayman's Bloody Bay Wall and on Grand Cayman's *Oro Verde*.

The male yellowhead jawfish performs the serious Mr. Mom duty of incubating eggs in its mouth.

Nassau groupers are so tame at several Cayman sites that they follow divers around like little puppies.

PHOTO CENTERS
The Cayman Islands provide ideal conditions for underwater video and still photography. Clear water, plentiful sunlight, current-free conditions and loads of exciting subjects attract beginners and veterans alike.

More than 20 Cayman operators rent underwater cameras. Still equipment rentals include Nikonos and Sea and Sea cameras, wide-angle lenses, strobes and close-up accessories. Photo instruction (from a few hours to week-long) and film processing for slides and prints, are offered on all three islands. Flooded and malfunctioning underwater cameras also can be handled at photo operations on any of the islands.

Video enthusiasts can rent housed systems and do it themselves, or opt to hire an underwater videographer specializing in custom shoots.

Jawfish

Yellowhead jawfish (*Opistognathus aurifrons*) are burrowing fish typically found in sandy, coral rubble areas near the reef. Since they reach only about 2 inches (5 cm) in length and are somewhat pale in coloration, most divers never even notice them. Look for a tan or pale blue body with dark eyes and a yellow head with bulldog jaws. They like to hover in a vertical position an inch or so above the bottom. Jawfish can be easily approached to within a few feet if you move slowly and smoothly. Be on the lookout for the male yellowheads with their mouths crammed full of tiny incubating eggs. Jackson's Bay in Little Cayman is an area that's loaded with jawfish.

Moray Eels

Some of the most respected residents of the reef are the moray eels. Their snake-like appearance and large toothy jaws can be intimidating to the novice. But in actuality, morays are not at all aggressive (unless food is in sight). Morays hide by day in crooks and crevices. At night, they freely roam. Several moray eel species are found on Cayman reefs. The **spotted morays** (*Gymnothorax moringa*) are the most common. They have dark brown spots on a pale body and reach lengths of around 3 feet (1 m). **Green morays** (*Gymnothorax funebris*) are the grand-daddies of the moray species. These green or brown eels can reach lengths of 6 feet (2 m) or more.

This coney is in its dramatic "golden phase" which is the least common of their various color phases.

Southern stingrays, smaller cousins of sharks and mantas, are the main attraction of the Stingray City site off Grand Cayman, but can be seen in shallow sandy areas off all of the islands.

Spotted eagle rays are usually seen cruising the walls, but are sometimes seen foraging in shallow, sandy areas for crustaceans and mollusks.

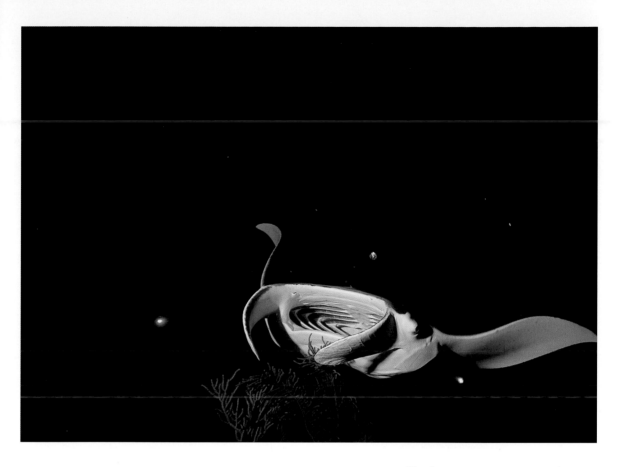

The famous manta ray named "Molly" was a favorite resident of Little Cayman for almost five years. She would swoop in and feed on the plankton attracted to diver's lights. Though Molly has been seen offshore, she has not approached divers since 1995. If and when she returns, be sure to treat her in a nonthreatening manner.

Waldo's Reef and the *Oro Verde* have resident green morays and there's Bruce, the green moray at Stingray City. **Goldentail morays** (*Gymnothorax miliaris*) are small, reaching only about 2 feet (62 cm) maximum. They have golden spots on a brown body with a yellow-tipped tail. The **chain moray** (*Echidna catenata*) is another small species that is dark brown with yellow chain markings. This rare species can be found at Disneyland in Little Cayman. The **purplemouth moray** (*Gymnothorax vicinus*) has a brownish body with bright yellow eyes.

Rays

Stingrays, eagle rays and manta rays—in the Caymans, you'll see them all! **Southern stingrays** (*Dasyatis americana*) are fairly common throughout the Caribbean, but in Grand Cayman they're a phenomenon. The tame, hand-fed rays at Stingray City are world famous. Divers flock to the North Sound where they can experience the soft touch of these hungry puppies. Southern stingrays are flat and disc-shaped and have a long, whiplike tail. Their top surface is gray or light brown and their undersides are pale. They are bottom feeders that normally feed on worms, mollusks

Tarpon, easily identified by their bulldog jaws and huge silvery scales, are strong swimmers that congregate at several Cayman sites bearing their namesake. Their average length is 4 feet (1.2 m), but they have been known to reach 8 feet (2.4 m).

and crustaceans. When not feeding, stingrays tend to hide under a cover of sand on the bottom. Over a period of time, the North Sound stingrays have been conditioned for feeding by divers. Squid and ballyhoo, a small beaked baitfish, are their favorites. The rays know if you have food and will politely bump and rub against you for a handout. As they pass by, gently stroke their bodies. Unlike their shark cousins, southern stingrays have smooth, velvety soft skin.

Alantic manta rays (*Manta birostris*) feed on plankton. They are also much larger, and being pelagic, are a somewhat rare encounter. A manta experience is always special, even for well-traveled veteran divers. Manta rays are flat and have enormous delta-shaped wings.

Adults reach widths of more than 20 feet (6 m). Their upper bodies are dark brown and their undersides are pale with gray or black blotches. They have large cephalic frontal fins that look like horns when furled. With the fins extended, mantas can steer or direct planktonic crustaceans and small fish into their wide mouths.

Mantas are known to initiate interaction with divers. For five years, a female manta named Molly fascinated hundreds of divers at Little Cayman. Molly was seen regularly along the sand flats at Jackson's Bay during night dives, but was last seen in the fall of 1995.

The majestic **spotted eagle rays** (*Aetobatus narinari*) are commonly seen cruising along the Cayman walls. Easily recognized by their

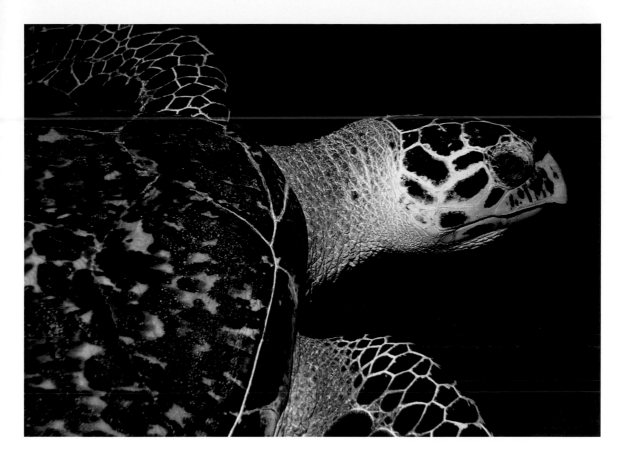

Hawksbill sea turtles like to feast on thimble jellyfish, tunicates, sponges, shrimp and even small squid. They are commonly seen in the Caymans patrolling around the shallow reefs and along the shoreline at Seven Mile Beach. Their carapace can reach a length of over 3 feet (1 m).

distinct leopard-like spots, eagle rays are extremely shy and normally stay at a distance. From afar, eagle rays are readily identified by their extra-long and slender tails.

In Grand Cayman, eagle rays can be seen along any of the walls, but are more frequently spotted flying along the North and East Walls. Favorite sites for encountering eagle rays include Leslie's Curl and Eagle Ray Pass. For a guaranteed eagle ray encounter, make a dusk dive or snorkel around the piers at one of the Cayman Brac resorts. Eagle rays are also common at Bloody Bay Wall in Little Cayman. There are several shallow sandy spots inside the Jackson's Bay Wall where they routinely feed on the mollusks and can be approached closely by divers.

Tarpon

Tarpon (*Megalops atlanticus*) are the kings of sport fish. They grow up to 8 feet (2.5 m) in length and look like giant, silvery herrings with pronounced, upturned jaws. Tarpon have huge, shiny scales. They have a single dorsal fin with a long, ribbon-like trailing fin. These extremely fast swimmers reach weights of more than 350 pounds (159 kg). They feed on small bait fish and are especially attracted to schooling silversides. Tarpon can be spotted at a number of Grand Cayman sites, such as Bonnie's Arch, Big Tunnel, Devil's Grotto, Soto's Reef, the original Tarpon Alley off the southwest shore, as well as the more familiar Tarpon Alley located just inside the North

Sound's Main Channel. Dozens of "silver kings" are also seen regularly at a number of East End sites, such as Grouper Grotto, Chub Hole, Snapper Hole, Kent's Caves, Ironshore Caves and Frank's Sound Gardens. Tarpon Reef off the south shore of Cayman Brac and Windsock Reef in Little Cayman are other popular tarpon hangouts.

Turtles

Turtles are gentle, air-breathing reptiles. Along with certain snakes and iguanas, turtles are one of the very few marine-adapted reptiles on earth.

Fossil records of sea turtles date back 200 million years when they lived in the era of dinosaurs. Three of the world's eight species presently inhabit the Cayman Islands. The **green** turtles (*Chelonia mydas*) are by far the most common in the Caymans. Along with the hawksbills, green turtles are the most tropical of the sea turtles. They have a relatively small, blunt-shaped head and an oval-shaped, olive-brown carapace (upper shell) with a pattern of dark, radiating streaks. The lower edge of their jaw is serrated and their flippers have one visible claw. Green turtles get their name from the coloration of their meat which is a highly sought after source of protein. They feed primarily on sea grasses and algae. Most adults weigh between 300 to 350 pounds (136-159 kg).

The smaller **hawksbill** turtle (*Eretmochelys imbricata*) has a protruding upper jaw that resembles a hawk's beak. Their carapace is relatively narrow and elliptical-shaped and is by far the most colorful of the sea turtles. The red, yellow and brown patterned shiny shells are used for jewelry, combs and inlays.

Hawksbills are carnivorous and feed on sponges, corals and tunicates. Adult hawksbills typically weigh between 100 and 200 pounds (46-91 kg).

The **loggerhead** turtles (*Caretta caretta*) can attain a weight of more than 350 pounds (159 kg). They are easily recognized by their heart-shaped carapace and huge, boxy heads. Front flippers are relatively short and thick and have two claws. Adults have a reddish-brown shell whereas the hatchlings are a darker brown. Loggerheads are carnivores and use their strong horny beaks to feed on crustaceans and occasionally on sea urchins and jellyfish.

All turtles are protected in Cayman waters including the pelagic **leatherbacks** (*Dermochelys coriacea*) and **olive ridley's** (*Lepidochelys olivacae*) that occasionally pass through. Because of their endangered status, turtle poducts are prohibited in most countries including the United States.

Turtles nest on the beach leaving a clutch of about 100 eggs unattended and vulnerable to predation. Their eggs look like small ping-pong balls and they incubate for about two months. After hatching, the baby turtles head to sea. The initial survival rate can be as low as 50 percent. Little is known of their whereabouts from that point until about a year later when they reach a juvenile size.

There's a chance of seeing a turtle at just about any Cayman site. Especially good sites for spotting turtles on Grand Cayman are Tarpon Alley, Orange Canyon and Kent's Caves. Strawberry Wall in Cayman Brac and Bloody Bay Wall in Little Cayman are also good bets for encountering turtles. Swimmers and snorkelers at Seven Mile Beach often see turtles swimming along the shoreline early in the day.

Appendix 1

Emergency Numbers

Hospital   **555 or 911**
George Town
Grand Cayman

Hospital   **555 or 948-2243/5**
Cayman Brac

Hyperbaric Chamber   **555**
Grand Cayman

Police   **911**

Divers Alert Network (DAN)   **(919) 684-8111**

Divers Alert Network (DAN)

The Divers Alert Network (DAN), a non-profit membership organization affiliated with Duke University Medical Center, operates a 24-hour emergency number **(919) 684-8111** (emergencies only) to provide divers and physicians with medical advice on treating diving injuries. DAN can also organize air evacuation to a recompression chamber.

Since many emergency room physicians do not know how to properly treat diving injuries, it is highly recommended that in the event of an accident, you have the physician consult a DAN doctor specializing in diving medicine.

All DAN members receive $100,000 emergency medical evacuation assistance and a subscription to the dive safety magazine, *Alert Diver.* New members receive the DAN *Dive and Travel Medical Guide* and can buy up to $125,000 of dive accident insurance.

DAN offers emergency oxygen first-aid training, and provides funding and consulting for recompression chambers worldwide. They also conduct diving research at Duke University's F.G. Hall Hyperbaric Center.

DAN's address is The Peter B. Bennett Center, 6 West Colony Place, Durham, NC 27705. Their non-emergency medical information number is (919) 684-2948. To join call (800) 446-2671.

APPENDIX 2

USEFUL NUMBERS

Cayman Islands Department of Tourism

Cayman Islands

P.O. Box 67
George Town
Grand Cayman, BWI
Tel: (345) 949-0623
Fax: (345) 949-4053

United States

Chicago
9525 W. Bryn Mawr, #160
Rosemont, IL 60018
Tel: (708) 678-6446
Fax: (708) 678-6675

Houston
Two Memorial City Plaza
820 Gessner, #170
Houston, TX 77024
Tel: (713) 461-1317
Fax: (713) 461-7409

Los Angeles
3440 Wilshire Blvd., #1202
Los Angeles, CA 90010
Tel: (213) 738-1968
Fax: (213) 738-1829

Miami
6100 Blue Lagoon Dr., #150
Miami, FL 33126-2085
Tel: (305) 266-2300
Fax: (305) 267-2932

New York
420 Lexington Ave., #2733
New York, NY 10172
Tel: (212) 682-5582
Fax: (212) 986-5123

Canada

Travel Marketing Consultants
234 Eglinton Ave. E., #306
Toronto, ON, M4P 1K5
Tel: (416) 485-1550
Fax: (416) 485-7578

United Kingdom

6 Arlington St.
London SW1A 1RE
Tel: (0171) 491-7771
Fax: (0171) 409-7773

Cycling

Cayman Cycle Rentals	945-4021
Eagle Nest Cycles	949-4866
McLaughlin Rentals (Little Cayman)	948-1000
Soto Scooters	945-4652

Golf

Britannia Golf Club	949-8020
The Links at SafeHaven	949-5988

Government & Associations

Chamber of Commerce	949-8090
Goverment Administration Bldg.	949-7900
Hotel & Condominium Assoc.	945-4057
National Watersports Assoc.	945-5491
Natural Resources Unit	949-8469
Pirates Week Office	949-5078/5859
Restaurant Assoc.	949-8522
Sister Island Tourism Assoc.	948-1345
Watersports Operators Assoc.	949-8522

Horseback Riding

Blazing Trails	949-7360
Nicki's Beach Rides	949-4729

Marinas

Aquanauts at Morgan's Harbour	945-1954
Cayman Islands Yacht Club	945-4322
Harbour House Marina	947-1307/1881

Places of Interest

Botanic Park	947-9462
National Museum	949-8368
Turtle Farm	949-3893/4
Harquail Theatre	949-5477

APPENDIX 3

PHOTO CENTERS

Grand Cayman

Bob Soto's Photo Center
P.O. Box 1801
Tel: (800) 262-7686
Fax: (345) 949-2022

Don Foster's Ocean Photo Centre
P.O. Box 30240
Tel: (800) 833-4837
Tel: (345) 949-7181
Fax: (345) 945-5133

Fisheye Photographic Services
P.O. Box 30076
Tel: (345) 945-4209
Fax: (345) 945-4208

Parrot's Landing Photo Centre
P.O. Box 1995 GT
Tel: (345) 949-7884
Fax: (345) 949-0294

Underwater Photo Centre & Gallery
Sunset House
P.O. Box 479
Tel: (345) 949-7111
Fax: (345) 949-7101

Cayman Brac

Ed Beaty's Reef Photo & Video Center
P.O. Box 185
Tel: (345) 948-1340

Photo Tiara
Divi Tiara Beach Resort
Stake Bay
P.O. Box 238
Tel: (345) 948-7553
Fax: (345) 948-7316

Little Cayman

Ed Beaty's Reef Photo & Video Center
P.O. Box 185
Tel: (345) 948-1340

APPENDIX 4

DIVE OPERATORS

Grand Cayman

Ambassador Divers
P.O. Box 2396 GT
Tel: (345) 949-8839
Fax: (345) 949-8839

Aquanauts, Ltd.
P.O. Box 30147
Tel: (345) 945-1990
Fax: (345) 945-1991

Bob Soto's Diving, Ltd.
P.O. Box 1801
Tel: (345) 949-2022
Fax: (345) 949-8731

Calico Jack's Pirates Emporium
P.O. Box 1995 GT
Tel: (345) 949-4373
Fax: (345) 949-0294

Capital's Surfside
P.O. Box 30370 SMB
Tel: (345) 949-7330
Fax: (345) 949-8639

Capt. Marvin's Aquatics
P.O. Box 413
Tel: (345) 945-4590
Fax: (345) 945-5673

Cayman Dive College
P.O. Box 30780 SMB
Tel: (345) 949-4125
Fax: (345) 949-4125

Cayman Diving Lodge
P.O. Box 11
East End
Tel: (345) 947-7555
Fax: (345) 947-7560

Cayman Diving School
P.O. Box 1308
Tel: (345) 949-4729
Fax: (345) 949-4729

Cayman Marine Lab Ltd.
P.O. Box 30548
Tel: (345) 947-0849
Fax: (345) 945-5586

Celebrity Divers
P.O. Box 637 GT
Tel: (345) 949-3410

Clint Ebanks Scuba Cayman
P.O. Box 746
Tel: (345) 949-3873
Fax: (345) 949-6244

Crosby Ebanks C & G Watersports
P.O. Box 30084
Tel: (345) 945-4049
Fax: (345) 945-5994

Dive Inn Ltd.
P.O. Box 30975 SMB
Tel: (345) 949-4456
Fax: (345) 949-7125

Dive 'N Stuff
P.O. Box 30609 SMB
Tel: (345) 947-1314
Fax: (345) 947-2095

Divetech/Turtle Reef Divers
P.O. Box 31435 SMB
Tel: (345) 949-1700
Fax: (345) 949-1701

Dive Time Ltd.
P.O. Box 2106 GT
Tel: (345) 947-2339
Fax: (345) 947-3308

Divers Down
P.O. Box 1706 GT
Tel: (345) 945-1611
Fax: (345) 945-1611

Divers Supply
P.O. Box 1995 GT
Tel: (345) 949-7621
Fax: (345) 949-7616

Don Foster's Dive Cayman
P.O. Box 31486
Tel: (345) 945-5132
Fax: (345) 945-5133

Eden Rock Diving Center Ltd.
P.O. Box 1907
Tel: (345) 949-7243
Fax: (345) 949-0842

Fisheye
P.O. Box 30076
Tel: (345) 945-4209
Fax: (345) 945-4208

Indies Divers
P.O. Box 2070 GT
Tel: (345) 945-5025
Fax: (345) 945-5024

Neptune's Realm Divers
P.O. Box 30520 SMB
Tel: (345) 949-6444
Fax: (345) 949-4417

Nitrox Divers
P.O. Box 959 GT
Tel: (345) 945-2064

Ocean Frontiers
P.O. Box 30433
East End
Tel: (345) 947-7500
Fax: (345) 947-7500

Off the Wall Divers
P.O. Box 30176 SMB
Tel: (345) 947-7790
Fax: (345) 947-7790

Ollen Miller's Sun Divers
P.O. Box 30181
Tel: (345) 945-6606
Fax: (345) 945-6706

Parrots Landing
P.O. Box 1995
Tel: (345) 949-7884
Fax: (345) 949-0294

Peter Milburn's Dive Cayman
P.O. Box 596
Tel: (345) 945-5770
Fax: (345) 945-5786

Quabo Divers
P.O. Box 157 GT
Tel: (345) 945-4769
Fax: (345) 945-4978

Red Sail Sports
P.O. Box 31473 SMB
Tel: (345) 945-5965
Fax: (345) 945-5808

Resort Sports Limited
P.O. Box 903
Tel: (345) 949-8100
Fax: (345) 945-5167

Rivers Sport Divers Ltd.
P.O. Box 374
West End
Tel: (345) 949-1181
Fax: (345) 949-1296

Scuba Sensations
P.O. Box 30188 SMB
Tel: (345) 949-2871
Fax: (345) 949-8731

Seasports
P.O. Box 431
West Bay
Tel: (345) 949-3965

7-Mile Watersports
P.O. Box 30742 SMB
Tel: (345) 949-0332
Fax: (345) 949-0331

Soto's Cruises
P.O. Box 30192
Tel: (345) 945-4576
Fax: (345) 945-1527

Sunset Divers
P.O. Box 479
Tel: (345) 949-7111
Fax: (345) 949-7101

Tortuga Divers Ltd.
P.O. Box 496 GT
East End
Tel: (345) 947-2097
Fax: (345) 947-9486

Treasure Island Divers
P.O. Box 30975
Tel: (345) 949-4456
Fax: (345) 949-7125

Liveaboards

Cayman Aggressor III
P.O. Box 1882G
Tel: (345) 949-5551
Fax: (504) 384-0817
Book through:
Aggressor Fleet Ltd.,
P.O. Drawer K,
Morgan City, LA 70381
(800) 348-2628

Submarines

Atlantis Submarines
P.O. Box 1043 GT
Tel: (345) 949-7700
Fax: (345) 949-8574

Cayman Brac

Brac Aquatics Ltd.
P.O. Box 89
West End
Tel: (345) 948-1429
Fax: (345) 948-1572

Peter Hughes Dive Tiara
Divi Tiara Beach Hotel
P.O. Box 238
Stake Bay
Tel: (345) 948-1553
Fax: (345) 948-1563

Reef Divers
Brac Reef Beach Resort
P.O. Box 56
West End
Tel: (345) 948-1323
Fax: (345) 948-1207

Liveaboards

Little Cayman Diver II
P.O. Box 280058
Tampa, FL 33682-0058
(800) 458-2722
Tel: (813) 932-1993
Fax: (813) 935-2250

Little Cayman

Paradise Divers
P.O. Box 42
Tel: (345) 948-0004
Fax: (345) 948-0004

Pirates Point Resort
Tel: (345) 948-1010
Fax: (345) 948-1011

Reef Divers Little Cayman Beach Resort
Blossom Village
Tel: (813) 323-8727
Fax: (813) 323-8827

Sam McCoy's Fishing & Diving Lodge
North Side
Tel: (345) 948-0026
Fax: (345) 948-0057

Southern Cross Club
P.O. Box 44
South Hole Sound
Tel: (317) 948-1099
Fax: (317) 948-1098

INDEX

A **boldface** page number denotes a picture caption.
An underlined page number indicates detailed treatment.